TABLE OF CONTENTS

Page

ACRONYMS

ACTIV	Army Concept Team in Vietnam
AID	Agency for International Development
AIT	Army Information Team
APC	Accelerated Pacification Campaign
APT	Armed Propaganda Team
ARVN	Army of the Republic of Vietnam
BATT	British Army Training Team
BRIAM	British Advisory Mission
CAO	Civic Affairs Office
CAT	Civic Action Team
COIN	Counterinsurgency
CORDS	Civil Operations and Revolutionary Development Support
CORDS/POD	Civil Operations and Revolutionary Development Support/Psychological Operations Division
CTZ	Corps Tactical Zone
DLF	Dhofar Liberation Front
DRV	Democratic Republic of Vietnam
EDCOR	Economic Development Corps
GVN	Government of Vietnam
HUMINT	Human Intelligence
IIBG	Imperial Iranian Battle Group
JUSMAG	Joint United States Military Assistance Group
JUSPAO	Joint United States Public Affairs Office

MAAG	Military Assistance and Advisory Group
MACV	Military Assistance Command Vietnam
MILDEC	Military Deception
MISB	Military Information Support Battalion
MISG	Military Information Support Group
MISO	Military Information Support Operations
NDFLOAG	National Democratic Front for Liberation of the Occupied Arabian Gulf
NLF	National Liberation Front
NRP	National Reconciliation Program
NVA	North Vietnamese Army
OCO	Office of Civil Operations
OSS	Office of Strategic Services
PDRY	Peoples Democratic Republic of Yemen
PF	Provincial Force
PFLO	Peoples Front for the Liberation of Oman
PFLOAG	Popular Front for the Liberation of the Occupied Arabian Gulf
PO	Psychological Operations Objective
POB	Psychological Operations Battalion
POG	Psychological Operations Group
POLWAR	Political Warfare
PPM	Psychological Warfare, Psychological Operations, and Military Information Support Operations
PSYACT	Psychological Action
PSYOP	Psychological Operations

PSYWAR	Psychological Warfare
PWB	Psychological Warfare Branch
PWD	Psychological Warfare Division
QR	Quick Reaction Request
RB&L	Radio Broadcast and Loudspeaker
RD	Revolutionary Development
RF	Regional Force
RVNAF	Republic of Vietnam Armed Forces
SAF	Sultan's Armed Forces
SAS	Special Air Service
SEP	Surrendered Enemy Personnel
SGA	Special Group, Augmented
SMM	Saigon Military Mission
TA	Target Audience
USIA	United States Information Agency
USIS	United States Information Service
VCI	Viet Cong Infrastructure
VIS	Vietnamese Information Service

ILLUSTRATIONS

CHAPTER 1

INTRODUCTION

> This is the so-called theory that "weapons decide everything," which constitutes a mechanical approach to the question of war and a subjective on-sided view. Our view is opposed to this; we see not only weapons but also people. Weapons are an important factor in war, but not the decisive factor; it is people, not things, that are decisive.
>
> — Mao Tse-Tung, *On Protracted War*

Insurgency is an irregular method of conducting warfare against an established state or government. Militarily inferior to the state, insurgency movements lack the necessary might to directly usurp governmental power and thus rely on indirect and protracted approaches. To facilitate the approaches, insurgents reach out to the population for political, logistical, and operational support, and often insurgents employ agitation, terrorism, and psychological warfare to obtain the required support. Understanding the insurgents' dependency on the population, governmental forces or "counterinsurgents" undertake specialized measures to separate the insurgents from the population's support.[1] These measures include a combination of military, economic, civic, political, and psychological aspects.[2] Taken together, the counterinsurgent effort is meant to achieve

---

[1]Censuses, identification cards, traffic control points, ration stamps, travel passes, curfews, educational policies, land reform, agricultural initiatives, and propaganda campaigns are all common tactics and techniques applied to deny insurgents support from the population. See Roger Trinquier, *Modern Warfare: A French View of Counterinsurgency*, trans. by Daniel Lee (Westport, CT: Praeger Security International), 2006), 36-42, 61-63.

[2]The US Army defines counterinsurgency as: "Those military, paramilitary, political, economic, psychological, and civic actions taken by a government to defeat insurgency." Department of the Army, Field Manual (FM) 1-02, *Operational Terms and Graphics* (Washington, DC: Government Printing Office, 2004), 1-47.

more than the destruction of the insurgent force but also to overcome the conditions that enable the insurgency.

Each of the aspects of counterinsurgency (COIN): military, economic, civic, etc., contributes to the combined effort although the weighting of each varies with the circumstances of the conflict. One of the aspects nonetheless constantly remains vital, and that aspect is psychological warfare (PSYWAR).[3] Successful PSYWAR is essential in countering insurgency.

Not to be misleading, PSYWAR by itself accomplishes nothing. However, when applied in conjunction with the multiple other aspects of a COIN operation, PSYWAR exponentially increases the collective effect. This is because PSYWAR is the one aspect of a COIN operation which enables, enhances, and exploits the other aspects. That being stated, trends in recent efforts at countering insurgencies suggest a lack of PSYWAR emphasis or even a lack of effectiveness relative to PSYWAR application.[4] This de-emphasis may be the result of deviations from established PSYWAR practices that have proven successful in previous counterinsurgencies. De-emphasis may also stem from the loss of particular lessons that made the established PSYWAR practices effective. On the other end of the spectrum, the de-emphasis also may be relative to the failure of

---

[3]The term psychological warfare encompasses those efforts made to influence, by persuasion or coercion, an enemy force and those who provide support to that force to act in manners that contribute to their defeat. Psychological operations and military information support operations have similar definitions and are more specifically defined later in this chapter.

[4]In Chapter 2 of this thesis, the expanding and shrinking relationship between PSYWAR and COIN is examined in greater detail.

PSYWAR to adapt, update, or improve in order to remain an enabler, enhancer, and exploiter of modern counterinsurgency warfare.

The aim of this thesis is to affirm that effective PSYWAR is a prerequisite factor in successful COIN operations and those COIN operations that do not emphasize and effectively employ PSYWAR are likely to fail. In order to substantiate the claim, the scope of the thesis will establish that central "best practices" exist in PSYWAR support to counterinsurgency operations such as legitimizing the government, eliciting defection, and making known the hidden agendas of insurgent organizations. In addition, this thesis will also illustrate that "lessons lost" occurred in history and in US Army doctrine which made PSYWAR less effective in supporting counterinsurgency operations and which eventually led to the marginalization of PSYWAR in COIN doctrine and practices.

Research Questions

Acknowledging that PSYWAR (also Psychological Operations and Military Information Support Operations) has been historically utilized as a primary aspect of counterinsurgency operations, this thesis presents and answers four questions about the means. First, is PSYWAR (Psychological Operations and Military Information Support Operations) actually essential in counterinsurgencies? Second, what are the best historic practices associated with these in counterinsurgencies? Third, are there any psychological "lessons lost" from previous counterinsurgency efforts that could be of benefit today? Fourth and most crucial, based on the previous three questions, what is still missing in the US Army's contemporary applications in counterinsurgencies?

Research Methodology

The body of this thesis consists of three segments organized into five chapters. The first segment examines how COIN PSYWAR theories evolved and what key COIN theorists surmised about the role PSYWAR operations. The second segment studies how COIN PSYWAR theories have been applied. Two case studies are examined, the Dhofar Rebellion (1963-1975) and the US involvement in the Vietnam War (1965-1972). These two cases were picked as they represent opposite ends of the spectrum. Though occurring during the same period, the visibility, scale, and approaches to each COIN operation differed greatly. To explore and substantiate the segments, primary research is utilized where possible such as firsthand accounts from interviews, literary works, and period documents. Secondary sources are used as well when those sources provide information or perspective not available at a given period. The final segment draws on the previous two segments in order to draw conclusions and provide recommendations.

In Chapter 2, the origins of US Army COIN and PSYWAR doctrine is examined relative to current doctrine. The early versions of Field Manual (FM) 31-22, *U.S. Army Counterinsurgency Forces*, FM 31-16, *Counterguerrilla Operations*, FM 33-1, *Psychological Operations*, and FM 33-5, *Psychological Operations Techniques and Procedures* are juxtaposed with the contemporary FM 3-24, *Counterinsurgency*, FM 3-24.2, *Tactics In Counterinsurgency*, FM 3-05.301, *Psychological Operations Tactics, Techniques, and Procedures*, and FM 3-05.302, *Tactical Psychological Operations Tactics, Techniques, and Procedures*. This portion of the thesis in meant to determine how and why PSYWAR and COIN doctrine evolved and did that evolution improve COIN operations or merely change it.

4

Chapter 3 provides an overview of the COIN and PSYWAR theories of four twentieth century "practitioner-theorists." These four COIN practitioners, General Sir Frank Kitson, Sir Robert Thompson, David Galula, and Major General Edward Lansdale, all participated in multiple COIN operations throughout the Cold War era. Each was instrumental in campaign planning and operations. Equally as important, the part that makes them theorists as well each captured their experiences and theories on paper. Frank Kitson participated in five counterinsurgencies, ranging from Kenya to Northern Ireland. He authored several books on COIN, including his most notable *Low Intensity Operations*. Robert Thompson fought communist insurgents in Malaya and was also a key advisor to the South Vietnamese and United States during the Vietnam War. His *Defeating Communist Insurgency* and *No Exit from Vietnam* are now classic works. David Galula experienced several Far Eastern counterinsurgencies and served in the French Army during the Algerian Revolution. He authored *Counterinsurgency Warfare: Theory and Practice* which is cited as a key reference in the current US Army FM 3-24, *Counterinsurgency*. Edward Lansdale was America's premier Cold War counterinsurgent thinker, successfully advising the Philippine government during their Huk Rebellion and spearheading American involvement in South Vietnam. Lansdale published *In the Midst of Wars*, documenting his experiences. Each of the practitioner-theorists wrote extensively on how PSYWAR supports COIN.

The first case study, found in chapter 4, recounts the circumstances and actions of the Dhofar Rebellion which occurred in southern Oman. A lengthy communist insurgency, the rebellion was eventually foiled by British intervention. The operation was conducted out of the eyes of the public and with a minimal number of forces. Aggressive

5

military action, coupled with extensive civil and psychological actions eventually cut off the insurgents from their support. The war was one of the few where western interventionist forces successfully defeated a communist insurgency in the twentieth century.

The second case study, recounted in chapter 5, examines the US portion of the Vietnam War. The entire conflict, encompassing the first and second Indochina War, lasted some three decades; however, large scale US involvement took place over a seven year period starting in 1965. The Vietnam War was termed a "dual war," being both a counterinsurgency operation and a massive conventional war. In additional to being a dual war, the complexity of the war was monumental in its own right by being fought during the peak of the Cold War and amid great social and political turmoil in the US. In the midst of the complexity, US psychological warfare and operations were tested and implemented on a scale not seen before or since. Yet, the war ended unsuccessfully for the US and South Vietnamese.

The final chapter, chapter 6, provides conclusions and recommendations. The four research questions are answered in an attempt to provide a comprehensive look at PSYWAR operations in COIN. The result is recommendations of how current PSYWAR operations can be improved by building on the foundations laid in the past.

Terms and Definitions

Before proceeding into this study, an understanding of the commonly used terms and definitions involved must be established. During the past hundred years a variety of naming conventions have emerged to describe military psychological warfare operations.

The most common terms include: Propaganda,[5] Psychological Warfare (PSYWAR), Political Warfare (POLWAR), Psychological Operations (PSYOP), Psychological Actions (PSYACT), and most recently Military Information Support Operations (MISO).[6] Colloquial terms such as sykewar, paper bullets, word warfare, and the fourth fighting arm also emerged.[7] The evolution of terms is confusing as dates, countries of origin, users, and contexts can change meanings. For instance, in the US Army, the term MISO replaced PSYOP which replaced PSYWAR; however, PSYWAR also remained a subdivision of PSYOP. Likewise, although the US currently uses the term MISO, the United Kingdom (UK) and all North Atlantic Treaty Organization (NATO) partners continue to use PSYOP, again adding a level of inconsistency.[8]

---

[5]The term propaganda came about specifically with the advent of the printing press. The Gutenberg Press, created in 1440, spread literacy and literature to the masses. The printing press also assisted the Protestant Reformation to gain substantial support. In an attempt to combat the reformation, the Roman Catholic Church established the *Congregatio de Propaganda Fide* [Congregation for the Propagation of the Faith] in 1622. The *Congregatio* utilized the printing press to produce tracts and pamphlets for missionary work, advocating Catholic opinion. The propagation materials became known as "propaganda." Martin Manning, *Historical Dictionary of American Propaganda* (Westport, CT: Greenwood Press, 2004), xxvii, xxxiii.

[6]Office of the Secretary of Defense, memorandum dated 3 December 2010, Subject: Changing the Term Psychological Operations to Military Information Support Operations.

[7]Leo J. Margolin, *Paper Bullets: A Brief Story of Psychological Warfare in World War II* (New York: Froben Press, 1946), 96-97.

[8]The United Kingdom commonly abbreviates Psychological Operations as "PsyOps" versus "PSYOP."

This confusing dialogue is nothing new. When Brigadier General Robert A. McClure,[9] the founder of American PSYWAR, was confronted with the question of similar confusing terms over sixty years ago, he pragmatically stated, "Call it what you may, international information, propaganda, or psychological warfare, the responsibilities still rest with us."[10] Since then, names and definitions have evolved and expanded but the fundamental understanding of the substance of PSYWAR has remained relatively constant.

When examining PSYWAR operations in COIN specifically, the term PSYWAR in its most nascent definition, provides a succinct and applicable description. When asked to define psychological warfare in 1942, the Office of Strategic Services (OSS)[11] Supporting Committee provided a basic estimate of PSYWAR as:

> [Psychological warfare] is the coordination and use of all means, including moral and physical, by which the end is attained--other than those of recognized military operations, but including the psychological exploitation of the result of those recognized military actions--which tend to destroy the will of the enemy to

---

[9]Major General (MG) Robert A. McClure (1897-1957) was a psychological warfare and "special warfare" visionary and advocate. He commanded the Psychological Warfare Branch Division / Supreme Headquarters, Allied Expeditionary Force (PWD/SHAEF) during WWII, the Office of the Chief of Psychological Warfare (OCPW) in 1950, and founded the Psychological Warfare Center in 1952 at Fort Bragg, North Carolina. MG McClure was the originator of contemporary US MISO and was instrumental in the creation of US Army Special Forces.

[10]Alfred H. Paddock, Jr., *US Army Special Warfare, Its Origins, Psychological and Unconventional Warfare, 1941-1952* (Washington, DC: National Defense University Press, 1982), 56.

[11]The Office of Strategic Services (OSS), though a civilian organization, was the proponent for psychological warfare prior to the Psychological Warfare Branch (PWB) and Psychological Warfare Division (PWD) being established in 1943. The OSS was a quasi-military organization designed to work behind enemy lines, conducting sabotage, partisan warfare, and psychological warfare. Though disbanded after the Second World War, it was the forerunner of the Central Intelligence Agency (CIA).

achieve victory and to damage his political or economic capacity to do so; which tend to deprive the enemy of the support, assistance or sympathy of his allies or associates or of neutrals, or to prevent his acquisition of such support, assistance, or sympathy; or which tend to create, maintain, or increase the will to victory of our own people and allies to acquire, maintain, or to increase the support, assistance and sympathy of neutrals.

In short, this definition states PSYWAR is the cumulative psychological measures taken to destroy the enemy's will or capacity to fight and alienate him from his support structures.[12] The current definitions of PSYOP and MISO differ slightly, being broadened to accommodate a wider range of peacetime activities.[13] Throughout this thesis, the applicable term for the period and conflict are used where specificity is required to preserve the contextual definition; however, PSYWAR, PSYOP, MISO, and PsyOps should be understood to have generally the same meaning.[14] Where no one doctrinal term adequately describes the method or operation, due to the expanse of time covered or generalness of application, the non-doctrinal term and acronym of PSYWAR-PSYOP-MISO (PPM) is substituted in this thesis for the ease of reading.[15]

---

[12]Paddock, *US Army Special Warfare, Its Origins*, 11.

[13]The US Army defines Psychological Operations as, "planned operations to convey selected information and indicators to foreign audiences to influence their emotions, motives, objective reasoning, and ultimately the behavior of foreign governments, organizations, groups, and individuals," and Psychological Warfare as, "the planned use of propaganda and other psychological actions having the primary purpose of influencing the opinions, emotions, attitudes, and behavior of hostile foreign groups in such a way as to support the achievement of national objectives."

[14]Early references and many British references often use the acronym PsyOps for psychological operations.

[15]The term PPM has no historical or doctrinal precedent and is a construct only used in the context of this thesis. The term PPM is intended to lesson confusion over military psychological terms.

Apart from the psychological discourse, the terms Irregular Warfare (IW), Unconventional Warfare (UW), Foreign Internal Defense (FID), and Counterinsurgency are often informally used arbitrarily and have doctrinally evolved over time. The terms UW, FID, and COIN all have specific definitions in current US Army doctrine; however, IW does not. IW has been defined by the Department of Defense (DoD) in 2008 as "A violent struggle among state and non-state actors for legitimacy and influence of the relevant populations(s). Irregular warfare favors indirect and asymmetric approaches, though it may employ the full range of military and other capacities, in order to erode an adversary's power, influence, and will," and includes a variety of operations and activities such as "counterterrorism; unconventional warfare; foreign internal defense; counterinsurgency; and stability operations."[16] For the purposes of this thesis, then, IW is considered an umbrella term for indirect and protracted warfare of which UW, FID, and COIN are subsets.

The term most often misused in association with counterinsurgency is unconventional warfare (UW). By obvious reasoning, UW takes on the meaning of all warfare that is not conventional. This common understanding is doctrinally incorrect. UW is broadly defined by US Army doctrine contributing to its misunderstanding.[17] The

---

[16]Department of Defense Directive, Number 3000.07, dated 1 December 2008, Subject: Irregular Warfare (IW).

[17]In FM 1-02, *Operational Terms and Graphics*, UW is defined as "A broad spectrum of military and paramilitary operations, normally of long duration, predominately conducted by indigenous or surrogate forces that are organized, trained, equipped, supported, and directed by an external source. It includes guerilla warfare and other direct offensive, low visibility, covert or clandestine operations, as well as the indirect activities of subversion, sabotage, intelligence activities, and evasion and escape."

United States Special Operations Command (USSOCOM) defines UW more succinctly as "activities conducted to enable a resistance movement or insurgency to coerce, disrupt, or overthrow a government or occupying power by operating through or with an underground, auxiliary, and guerilla force in a denied area."[18] UW is then a specific term used for an operation with an aim that is the opposite of COIN, as compared to a general term describing all operations that are not conventional.[19]

The other term closely associated with COIN is FID. According to US Army doctrine, FID is defined as "participation by civilian and military agencies of a government in any of the action programs taken by another government to free or protect its society from subversion, lawlessness, and insurgency."[20] Although the doctrinal definition of FID is similar to the doctrinal definition of COIN, in practice FID refers to increasing the military capacity of a nation and may be conducted in support of a COIN operation.

With the common understanding established on the definitions of PPM, IW, UW, FID, and COIN, this thesis proceeds to examine the origins and doctrinal development of US PPM and COIN in the following chapter. The second chapter illustrates that in early

---

[18]Department of the Army, TC 18-01. *Special Forces Unconventional Warfare* (Washington, DC: Government Printing Office, 2011), 1-1.

[19]Although terms such as conventional warfare and conventional military forces appear consistently in US Army doctrine, including updated 2011 Army Doctrine Publications, no formal definition exists. For the purposes of this thesis conventional warfare refers to military combat operations conducted by general purpose forces with the aim of defeating an opposing national military force.

[20]Department of the Army, FM 1-02, 1-84.

US Army doctrine, PPM was considered essential in COIN; however, the PPM emphasis in COIN has eroded in contemporary doctrine.

CHAPTER 2

EVOLUTION OF US COIN AND PPM DOCTRINE

Although psychological operations may be effectively integrated to support
military actions in limited and general warfare, it is essential to the success in
both counterinsurgency and unconventional warfare.
— Field Manual 33-5, *Psychological Operations,*
Techniques, and Procedures (1966)

Brief History of US Psychological Warfare and Operations

The use of PPM is as old as warfare itself. Ancient military leaders such as the

Persian general Xerxes; the Carthaginian general Hannibal; and Mongol warlord Genghis

Khan, all employed PPM to great effect in their military endeavors.[21] Likewise, PPM has

been integral in US military endeavors since the American Revolution as evidenced in

sophisticated leaflets, handbills, and pamphlets produced during the period. For instance,

Thomas Paine's *Common Sense*, which greatly spurred patriotic fervor, was disseminated

as a series of pamphlets.[22] Not until the mid-twentieth century; however, did US military

PPM formalize in doctrine and application.

---

[21]Xerxes, Hannibal, and Ghenghis Khan each conducted psychological warfare as
an integral part of their military campaigns. Xerxes spread rumors of massive archer
formations to intimidate the Greeks. Hannibal sent messengers into Rome warning of a
secret weapon that could not be stopped, smashing Roman will to fight. Ghenghis Khan
creatively fed exaggerations to spies who returned home with tales of limitless hordes of
cavalry and solders so ferocious they dined on wolfs and bears. Paul M. A. Linebarger,
Psychological Warfare (Washington: Combat Forces Press, 1948), 3-5, 14-16; Leo J.
Margolin, *Paper Bullets: A Brief Story of Psychological Warfare in World War II* (New
York: Froben Press, 1946), 20.

[22]Ibid., 20-24.

PPM, primarily psychological warfare, was employed extensively in early

twentieth century warfare, including the First World War and the Central American wars

collectively known as the Banana Wars; each with varying degrees of organization,

formality, and effectiveness. In fact, the term psychological warfare originated in the

twentieth century when in 1920 British military historian J. F. C. Fuller wrote:

> This method of imposing the will of one man on another may in its turn be
> replaced by a purely psychological warfare, wherein weapons are not even used
> or battlefields sought or loss of life or limb aimed at; but, in place, the corruption
> of human reason, the dimming of human intellect, and the disintegration of the
> moral and spiritual life of one nation by the influence of the will of another is
> accomplished.[23]

Naturally PPM organizations existed in the First World War; the conflict is

known for its extensive propaganda. On the home front, the US Committee on Public

Information (CPI) stirred American passion.[24] Across the ocean, the Propaganda Section

of the G-2, General Headquarters, American Expeditionary Forces (GHQ/AEF),

conducted extensive propaganda operations, mostly in radio and leaflet. However, both

organizations were ad hoc creations and were dissolved following the armistice.[25]

The roots of modern PPM, and its relationship to counterinsurgency, were planted

in the Second World War. After thirteen years with no military PPM organizations in the

---

[23]J. F. C. Fuller, *Tanks in the Great War, 1914-1918* (London: John Murray, 1920), 320.

[24]The Committee on Public Information (CPI) should not be considered a psychological warfare organization as its target audience was the American people. However, it was intended to influence public opinion and generate support for American involvement in the First World War.

[25]Harold D. Lasswell, "Organization of Psychological Warfare Agencies in World War I," in *A Psychological Warfare Casebook*, eds. William E. Daugherty and Morris Janowitz (Bethesda, MD: The Johns Hopkins Press-Operations Research Office, 1958), 120-126; Linebarger, 62-70.

US military, Psychological Warfare Branches (PWB) were established in 1942 at army theater level, followed by the Psychological Warfare Division (PWD) in 1944. Additionally, the OSS took ownership of some aspects of PPM. Although all these organizations were disbanded, demobilized, or drawn down after the Second World War, an organizational skeleton continued to exist.[26] Also for the first time in US military history, a small cadre of experienced PPM professionals remained on active duty; whereas after the First World War, all PPM experience and continuity were lost.[27]

Of those experienced in PPM and remaining on active duty, two were instrumental in establishing US PPM capabilities and the relationship of PPM with COIN—Brigadier General (BG) Robert McClure and Colonel (COL) Russell Volckmann. McClure had commanded the PWD in the Second World War and remained an advocate for PSYWAR afterwards. Through his initiative, a Psychological Warfare Center was established at Fort Bragg, North Carolina in 1952 which he commanded.[28] The Psychological Warfare Center became the center for all irregular warfare and the US

---

[26]By 1947, only one operational psychological warfare organization remained in the US Army. Located at Fort Riley, Kansas, the Tactical Information Detachment was reflagged as the 1st Loudspeaker and Leaflet (L&L) Company in 1950 and formed the nucleus of psychological warfare capability during the Korean Conflict. It was closely followed by the 1st Radio Broadcasting and Leaflet (RB&L) Group, established and deployed to Korea in 1951. A staff organization was also created in 1950, the Office of the Chief of Psychological Warfare (OCPW). The OCPW was commanded by BG Robert McClure who had formerly commanded a PWB and the PWD. See Paddock, "U.S. Military Psychological Operations: Past, Present, and Future," 20-21.

[27]Paddock, "U.S. Military Psychological Operations: Past, Present, and Future," 20-21.

[28]BG McClure was later promoted to Major General. McClure retired from active duty in 1958 and died the following year.

Army Special Forces (SF) were formed under it at the same time.[29] COL Volckmann, who led guerrilla bands in the Philippines against the Japanese and authored the US Army's first counterguerrilla manual in 1951, was chosen to oversee the SF development.[30] Largely because of COL Volckmann's role in the new organization, the Psychological Warfare Center assumed responsibility for COIN capability and doctrine development shortly afterwards. Over the next decade, the center itself did not greatly increase in size or force structure but created a permanent platform for increasing irregular capabilities.

The next expansion of PPM capability came about as a result of the introduction of US combat troops into South Vietnam in 1965.[31] Starting with an ad hoc psychological operations battalion formed from separate companies, within three years, the force structure for PPM increased into two full active duty groups. These two groups, the 4th Psychological Operations Group (POG) and the 7th POG, operated in South Vietnam and also supported from Okinawa.[32]

---

[29]The Psychological Warfare Center included a PSYWAR School, the 6th Radio and Broadcasting Group, and the 10th Special Forces Group. It was later renamed the Special Warfare Center, the Center for Military Assistance, and the John F. Kennedy Special Warfare School and Center.

[30]COL Volckmann's FM 31-20, *Operations Against Guerrilla Forces* was the first modern US Army counterinsurgency manual and advised a holistic approach to counterguerrilla operations including "political, administrative, economic, and military policies, intelligently conceived, wisely execute, and supported by appropriate propaganda." Birtle, 134-135.

[31]The term PSYOP replaced the term PSYWAR in US Army doctrine in 1962.

[32]See chapter 5 of this thesis for greater detail on the 4th POG and 7th POG.

After the war, the force structure decreased again and the 4th POG became the only remaining active duty PPM capability in the US Army for the next forty years. Although organizational transformation occurred over those forty years, such as the establishment of the United States Army Special Operations Command (USASOC) in 1987 as the 4th POG's parent headquarters, PPM continuity was maintained.[33] Currently, PPM organization and continuity continues to evolve with the establishment of a provisional second active duty group in 2011. Consequentially, from 1952 to present, the US Army has maintained continuous and developing PPM capability.

PPM Doctrine Linked and Unlinked

Sixty years after the proponent for psychological warfare and counterinsurgency doctrine was established, doctrinal development for both should reflect significant integration of the two. Not so. When the US Army published FM 3-24, *Counterinsurgency* in 2006, it revitalized movement and thought on the subject. As stated in the foreword though, the manual provides a "general approach to counterinsurgency operations." This holds especially true for the psychological aspects of COIN, which are referenced repetitively yet vaguely in the manual. In fact, although included in the formal definition (Counterinsurgency includes the military, paramilitary, political, psychological, and civic actions taken by a government to defeat insurgency), and

---

[33]The 4th POG has now been reflagged as the 4th Military Information Support Group (MISG) due to the transition from the term PSYOP to the term MISO. In 2011, the 4th MISG (A) provisionally transformed into a Military Information Support Operations Command (MISOC), splitting into two groups yet retaining the same cumulative number of battalions. The second group, 8th MISG(A), provisionally activated in 2011. Each group contains three Military Information Support Battalions (MISB).

characterized as a "key counterinsurgency participant" and a "special requirement" in the manual, FM 3-24 provides no definitive role, function, or priority for PPM.[34]

The companion manual, FM 3-24.2, *Tactics in Counterinsurgency*, published in 2009, provides a minimal explanation of PPM application in COIN operations but only as a subheading under "Information Engagement." The manual directs psychological targeting of two universal target audiences, providing three key "facets" or simplified objectives for each.[35] However, no substantive discourse on integration, analysis, theory, method, purpose, role, or significance is addressed.[36]

Similarly, the current doctrine for PPM focuses on process, method and capabilities but contains no background or techniques for specifically supporting COIN. Although FM 3-05.301, *Psychological Operations Process, Tactics, Techniques, and Procedures*, published in 2007, and FM 3-05.302, *Tactical Psychological Operations Tactics, Techniques, and Procedures*, published with Change 1 in 2009, provide the intended base and structure for conducting PPM, the manuals are as general in COIN

---

[34]Department of the Army, Field Manual (FM) 3-24, *Counterinsurgency* (Washington, DC: Government Printing Office, 2006), 1-1, 2-5, 6-15, B-8.

[35]FM 3-24.2 states PPM should target the "population" to: obtain buy-in for actions that affect the populace; win over passive or neutral people by showing host nation legitimacy; and encourage locals to provide information about the insurgency to US or host nation security forces. PPM should also target the 'insurgents' to: divide insurgent leaders and guerrillas, divide insurgents and mass base, and create a means for insurgents to abandon the movement and return to society

[36]Department of the Army, Field Manual (FM) 3-24.2, *Tactics in Counterinsurgency* (Washington, DC: Government Printing Office, 2009), 4-11, 4-12.

substance as FM 3-24 is. In fact, the term "counterinsurgency" itself is not used in either manual.[37]

What makes this occurrence ironic is that the field manuals of the Cold War era heavily integrated PPM in COIN theory. For instance, though not termed COIN at the time, the first US Army counterinsurgency manuals published in 1951, FM 31-20, *Operations Against Guerrilla Forces* and FM 31-21, *Organization and Conduct of Guerrilla Warfare* considered PPM as one of the key elements in combating guerrillas and included discourse on application.[38] Likewise, FM 31-22, *US Army Counterinsurgency Forces*, published in 1963, included a chapter on PPM.[39] Rather than merely acknowledging PPM, as FM 3-24 appears to, or oversimplifying as FM 3-24.2 does, PPM theory and integration were highlighted in the earlier FM 31-20, FM 31-21 and FM 31-22. FM 31-22 even included bulletized psychological objectives similar to those found in the current FM 3-24.2, but also the publication provided the context and

---

[37]Although current PPM doctrinal publications (FM 3-05.30, *Psychological Operations*; FM 3-05.301, *Psychological Operations Process, Tactics, Techniques, and Procedures*; and FM 3-05.302, *Tactical Psychological Operations Tactics, Techniques, and Procedures*) contain minimal specificity on supporting COIN operations, future publications may return to placing emphasis on and providing detail for supporting COIN. The draft version of FM 3-53, *Military Information Support*, which will replace FM 3-05.30, contains some specificity for supporting COIN. The authorized version of FM 3-53 is expected to be published in 2012.

[38]Department of the Army, Field Manual (FM) 31-21, *Organization and Conduct of Guerrilla Warfare* (Washington, DC: Government Printing Office, 1951), 155.

[39]Department of the Army, Field Manual (FM) 31-22, *U.S. Army Counterinsurgency Forces* (Washington, DC: Government Printing Office, 1963), 10, 77-81.

reasoning behind them. Even the later FM 31-16, *Counterguerrilla Operations*, published in 1967, included the context of PPM purpose, concept, organization, and operation.[40]

Similarly, PPM doctrine of the period included theory on COIN. FM 33-5, *Psychological Operations Techniques and Procedures*, published in 1966, contained not only PPM process and procedure but also included a full chapter entitled "Psychological Operations in Countering Insurgency."[41] Covered in the chapter were topics on how PPM could support Nation Building Programs, Environmental Improvement Programs, Population and Resource Control Programs, and Counterguerrilla Operations as well how PPM could combat Subversive Insurgent Psychological Objectives and Subversive Insurgent Propaganda Organization.[42] Figures 1 and 2 illustrate this rise and fall of PPM emphasis in COIN doctrine and vice-versa, in general.

---

[40]Department of the Army, Field Manual (FM) 31-16, *Counterguerrilla Operations* (Washington, DC: Government Printing Office, 1967), 82-83.

[41]The 1955 version of FM 33-5, *Psychological Warfare Operations* addressed counterguerrilla operations but briefly.

[42]Department of the Army, Field Manual (FM) 33-5, *Psychological Operations Techniques and Procedures* (Washington, DC: Government Printing Office, 1966), 22-37.

FM 33-5 Psychological Warfare (1949)	FM 33-5 Psychological Warfare (1955)	FM 33-5 Psychological Operations (1962)	**FM 33-5 Psychological Operations Techniques (1966)**	FM 33-1 Psychological Operations (1968)
No reference to counter guerrilla operations	Brief address of counter guerrilla operations	First US Army manual to use the term "counter insurgency"	Detailed COIN Chapter: Nation Building, Environmental Improvement, P&R Control, Counter Guerrilla	Chapters on Stability Operations & Consolidation Operations
FM 33-1 Psychological Operations (1979)	FM 33-1-1 Psychological Operations Techniques & Procedures (1994)	FM 3-05.301 Psychological Operations Process, Tactics, Techniques & Procedures (2003)	FM 3-05.301 Psychological Operations Process, Tactics, Techniques & Procedures (2007)	FM 3-05.302 Tactical Psychological Operations TTPs (CHG 1, 2009)
Full chapters on PSYOP support to FID and UW	Some reference to COIN-basic objectives	Some reference to COIN-basic objectives	No reference to COIN	No reference to COIN (Some reference to FID)

NOTE: Only key PSYWAR/PSYOP/MISO manuals are illustrated. Manual with most definitive COIN discourse is highlighted.

Figure 1.   COIN emphasis in PSYWAR/PSYOP/MISO doctrine
Source: Created by author.

FM 31-21 Organization and conduct of Guerrilla Warfare (1951)	FM 31-16 Operations Against Irregular Forces (1961)	**FM 31-22 US Army Counter Insurgency Forces (1963)**	FM 31-16 Counter Guerrilla Operations (1967)	**FM 90-8 Counter Guerrilla Operations (1986)**	FM 3-24 Counter Insurgency (2007)
Small chapter on PSYWAR	Section on Propaganda	Thorough Chapter on PSYOP	Section on PSYOP	Improved Section on PSYOP: provides general tasks and background relevance	PSYOP/MISO discussion vague and minimal

NOTE: Only key Counter Guerrilla/COIN manuals are illustrated. Manuals with most definitive PSYWAR /PSYOP/ MISO discourse are highlighted.

Figure 2.   PSYWAR/PSYOP/MISO emphasis in COIN doctrine
Source: Created by author.

The contrast of PPM and COIN doctrine of the 1960s with PPM and COIN doctrine of the present age indicates one of two developments. It suggests (1) either that PPM was viewed as ineffective or irrelevant and intentionally marginalized in current doctrine or (2) current doctrine is lacking in addressing a "special requirement" appropriately. In situation, the detail and the purpose of PPM in support COIN in the 1960s has been deemphasized in post 2001 doctrine.

PPM Effects and Relevance

Part of the difficulty in determining if PPM remains relevant to COIN lies in the ability to accurately gauge effects. The effects of an artillery fire mission or an Air Force sortie are often instantly apparent and a direct cause-and-effect relationship is obvious. However, with PPM effects may take years to become observable and even then cause-and-effect relationships may be impossible to isolate. Occasionally, obvious effects are observed such as the case when 1,800 Chinese troops surrendered due to a C-47 aircraft loudspeaker broadcast in the Korean Conflict.[43] Other effects are quantifiably measurable such as during a two month period in Europe in 1944 where 25 percent of German prisoners of war had deserted and of those deserters, 90 percent had safe-passage leaflets in their possession.[44] While a number of surrenders can be counted, many objectives in a COIN environment cannot be measured. For instance, how can the action of village elders refusing to provide aid to an insurgent group be identified and verified? Consequently, the failure of PPM to influence target audiences may not lead to

---

[43]Paddock. *US Army Special Warfare*, 94.

[44]Margolin, 104.

irrelevance but rather the failure to identify, isolate, and verify the effects. In fact, PPM

theorist Paul Linebarger noted this phenomenon in his classic 1948 *Psychological*

Warfare work:

> Psychological warfare is waged before, during, and after war; it is not waged
> against the opposing psychological warfare operators; it is not controlled by the
> laws, usages, and customs of war; and it cannot be defined in terms of terrain,
> order of battle, or named engagements. It is a continuous process. Success or
> failure is often known only months or years after the execution or the operation.
> Yet success, though incalculable, can be overwhelming; and failure, though
> undetectable, can be mortal.[45]

The Shortcoming of COIN and PPM Doctrine: Consensus

Doctrine is obviously a valuable tool to counterinsurgent forces. The theory of

developed from the accumulated experiences of multiple perspectives can guide and

shape effective COIN operations. The strength of doctrine though is also its weakness as

cumulative experiences require consensus to become doctrine. Consensus often takes the

edge off innovative theory. The insight of knowledgeable and experienced individuals

can also guide effective operations just as authoritatively as doctrine. The following

chapter attempts to accomplish this: examine the COIN and PPM theories of

knowledgeable and experienced individual counterinsurgents who were not consensus

builders but innovators. Each of these innovative counterinsurgents considered PPM as

paramount in a comprehensive COIN strategy.

---

[45]Linebarger's book, *Psychological Warfare*, was widely read by the PPM
practitioners of the Cold War era and influenced their thinking. Of note, two US Cold
War COIN practitioners discussed in the following chapter, Edward Lansdale and Rufus
Phillips, both used the work to gain an understanding of PPM and guide their efforts in
the Philippines and Vietnam. See Linebarger. *Psychological Warfare*, 1.

CHAPTER 3

THE CLASSIC COUNTERINSURGENTS AND PPM

It is only necessary to stress once again that wars of subversion and counter subversion are fought, in the last resort, in the minds of people, for the importance of a good psychological operations organization to become apparent.
— Frank Kitson, *Low Intensity Operations*

A person who has been persuaded to do nothing can very soon be persuaded, by blackmail if necessary, to do something which puts him irrevocably under insurgent control.
— Robert Thompson, *Defeating Communist Insurgency*

If there was a field in which we were definitely and indefinitely more stupid than our opponents, it was propaganda.
— David Galula, *Pacification in Algeria*

Use psychological warfare--psywar--to trick, harass, and confuse an enemy, to raise his fears, to expose his weaknesses. It is an important component of any campaign against insurgents. Be willing to try the unconventional. An army must comport itself not only with military alertness but with psychological insights.
— Edward Lansdale, *Edward Lansdale, the Unquiet American*

Why Study the Classic Counterinsurgents Views of PPM?

During the twentieth century, a unique mixture of ideologies, technologies, and socio-economic conditions occurred initiating an unprecedented level of irregular warfare. In the midst of these circumstances, a number of counterinsurgency experts emerged who had fought to counter these insurgencies and had time to reflect on their efforts. As a result, several of these scholarly warriors can be considered Classic Counterinsurgents-combining academic study, first hand experiences, and writing extensively on the theories formed from both.

In the context of this thesis, four classic counterinsurgents are considered especially noteworthy: Frank Kitson, Robert Thompson, David Galula, and Edward

24

Lansdale. Each participated in multiple counterinsurgency operations, at various levels of command, and produced the writings that directly affected the tactics of militaries and the strategies of nations. Though many others have provided extensive thought on insurgency and counterinsurgency, these four are uniquely qualified to be considered the classics.[46]

A key aspect of in each of their counterinsurgency theories is the application of PPM to support comprehensive operations. All of the stated foundational counterinsurgents considered PPM imperative to a counterinsurgency campaign and included their views for the use and goals of the aspect in their writings. An examination of these original works, free from the interpretations of intermediary scholars, provides insight in detail and specificity for the use of PPM in current counterinsurgencies.

General Sir Frank Kitson

Serving over forty years in the British Army, General Sir Frank Kitson served in five separate wars providing an unparalleled breadth of experience to formulate counterinsurgency theory. Commissioning three years after the end of World War II, Kitson was involved in several key Cold War counterinsurgencies and peace keeping operations during the 1950s and early 1960s including the Mau Mau Rebellion in Kenya, the Malayan Emergency, the Muscat and Oman Rebellion, and the Cyprus Problem. He

---

[46]A number of other counterinsurgents could be considered classic. In terms of prevailing contribution to multiple conflicts though, these four stand out. All four experienced both successful and unsuccessful counterinsurgencies: Kitson-Oman and Northern Ireland (note the Northern Ireland operation was considered successful in the end but during the period of Kitson's involvement the war was generally not going well for the counterinsurgent forces); Thompson-Malaya and Vietnam; Galula-Greece and Algeria; and Lansdale-Philippines and Vietnam. In addition, all four published books that were influential in shaping counterinsurgency thought and efforts beyond their time of service.

also commanded a brigade in Northern Ireland during the early 1970s before being promoted to the most senior army positions.[47]

Over the years, Kitson authored several books derived from his experiences, articulating foundational counterinsurgency theory. Kitson published *Gangs and Counter-gangs* in 1960; *Low Intensity Operations: Subversion, Insurgency, Peace-Keeping,* in 1971; *Bunch of Five* in 1977; and lastly *Warfare as a Whole* in 1987 after his retirement from active duty. The works, primarily *Low Intensity Operations* and *Bunch of Five*, provide experienced insight on warfare and more specifically narrate his thoughts on the importance and application of PPM in countering insurgencies.

An array of experiences, ideas, and reflections are contained in Kitson's writings. The paramount argument he conveyed though is the difference between combating a conventional threat and combating an insurgency. Whereas in conventional warfare the destruction of the enemy force is the primary aim, the aim of the insurgent or counterinsurgent is to gain a sizable enough allegiance of the population to sway the conflict, sizable enough to uphold the government or sizable enough to overthrow the government, Kitson related. Likewise, he concluded that the use of force to destroy the enemy becomes a subordinate effort to gaining and maintaining the loyalty of the population that enables or disables the insurgent's goals. In Kitson's own words:

> the main characteristic which distinguishes campaigns of insurgency from other forms of war is that they are primarily concerned with the struggle for men's

---

[47]The Mau Mau Rebellion occurred from 1952 to 1960 in Kenya; the Malayan Emergency occurred from 1948 to 1960; the Muscat and Oman Rebellion occurred from 1957 to 1959; the Cyprus Problem occurred roughly between 1963 and 1967 though incidents of organized violence predated and followed; and Northern Ireland occurred roughly from 1968 to 1980. See Frank Kitson, *Bunch of Five* (London: Faber and Faber Limited, 1977).

minds, since only by succeeding in such a struggle with a large enough number of people can the rule of law be undermined and constitutional institutions be overthrown. Violence may play a greater or lesser part in the campaign, but it should be used very largely in the support of ideas.[48]

Key in this struggle for men's minds, as Kitson conveys, is the conduct of PPM and he writes extensively on the subject.

In Kitson's most famous work, *Low Intensity Operations*, he discusses the application of PPM, providing the purpose, the technical process, some tactics, and the makeup of effective PPM organizations. According to Kitson, the principle purpose of PPM is to present the attributes of the established government in a manner that is desirable to the population and conversely countering and discrediting the appeals of the insurgent force.[49] Governments that fail to establish their attributes as offering beneficial superiority therefore lack reasonable appeal. Kitson described the mechanical process behind promoting the government and discrediting the insurgents in three aspects. To begin with, detailed assessments of the population and circumstances are made by specially trained personnel. The assessments are then developed into PPM programs and once accepted by appropriate government officials are made policy. The programs' arguments are conveyed in products such as leaflets, print articles, radio, and films which are disseminated to the population.[50] Of note, though communicated in broad terms, the

---

[48]Kitson, *Bunch of Five*, 282.

[49]Frank Kitson, *Low Intensity Operations: Subversion, Insurgency, Peace-Keeping* (London: Faber and Faber Limited, 1971), 77.

[50]Ibid.

mechanical process Kitson described in 1971 mirrors that of the United States Army's current doctrine in use today, specifically Phases II through VI of the PPM process.[51]

In the writing, Kitson described one key technique in achieving primary purpose: exposing the underlying motives of insurgent forces and discrediting the insurgent organization using the true yet undesirable aspects of the insurgent agenda. He suggested insurgent groups often obscure their principal aspirations and promote only selected portions or alternate forms of their agenda in order to gain acceptance from a broader audience. An example he provided is the Indo-Chinese Communist Party's promotion of nationalism to combat the Japanese, and later the French, knowing the promotion of communism would not be accepted as enthusiastically. Based on this, he argued, by identifying and making known the "veiled aims," the moderate segment of the population may withhold commitment, degrading and possibly isolating insurgent support mechanisms.[52]

An organizational template and organizational peculiarities for PPM units supporting counterinsurgency operations are also included in the work. About organization, Kitson stated that each level of command should be supported by an

---

[51]Steps 2 through 6 of the process are Target Audience Analysis; Series Development; Product Development and Design; Approval; and Production, Distribution, and Dissemination. Steps 3 through 6 are self explanatory; Step 2 is the most crucial as it lays the foundation. Target Audience Analysis (TAA) identifies key target audiences (TA); determines if the TA can conduct the desired behavior; evaluates the conditions the TA lives in and deals with; determines vulnerabilities in the TA to stimulate the desired action; determines if the TA is likely to response to persuasion; determines how the TA can be accessed; develops arguments; and determines how to assess effectiveness. See Department of the Army, Field Manual (FM) 3-05.301, *Psychological Operations Process Tactics, Techniques, and Procedures* (Washington, DC: Government Printing Office, 2007).

[52]Kitson, *Low Intensity Operations,* 84-85.

operational team capable of conducting assessments, providing advice to commanders, and developing and disseminating propaganda while operating within centralized parameters. The teams should be capable of conducting interpersonal face-to-face influence in directed areas as well. In addition, Kitson offered two peculiarities for PPM organizations: the organizations must rely on indigenous advisors and civilian personnel may form the organization itself. No foreign military propagandist, no matter how much of an expert on a region, possesses the same degree of cultural, historical, and geographic knowledge as natives do, argued Kitson. Therefore, exploiting indigenous talent in the analysis of a population and in the development of PPM is essential. He also argued that an army may not always need to provide the core of a PPM organization and cases exist, like the civilian Information Service used during the Malayan Emergency, where effective PPM organizations could be staffed by civilians. Kitson caveats this though by acknowledging the time required to build such an organization may be substantial and only an army has the capability of maintaining readily available, adequately trained, and experienced PPM units.[53]

Apart from organization, Kitson addressed the timelines associated with PPM activities. Knowing political agitation generally precedes militant aspects of an insurgency, such as guerilla warfare and terrorism, he advocated conducting PPM as early in a campaign as possible. Kitson stated that although governmental progress may occur at the onset of an insurgency, it fails to reach full potential with the population

---

[53]Ibid., 77-79.

unless exploited through PPM. This is the core of the Kitson's concern for a military

PPM unit as opposed to a civilian led agency.[54]

In a following work, *Bunch of Five,* Kitson elaborated on the use of PPM in the

context of counterinsurgency framework. Kitson used the analogy of a picture frame to

describe his overall theory for an effective counterinsurgency campaign and described

PPM as being fundamental in enabling one side of the frame. The four sides of Kitson's

counterinsurgency campaign frame are the coordinating machinery, intelligence, law, and

the political atmosphere. The coordinating machinery synchronizes the efforts of all

governmental, non-governmental, and military organizations to ensure all operations are

de-conflicted and work towards centralized goals. Intelligence facilitates understanding

of insurgent organizations, provides background and contact information, and enables

interdiction or exploitation. Law supports the legitimacy and justness of the government

and military counterinsurgency force in national and international venues. Lastly, the

political atmosphere, according to Kitson, generates a receptive response of the

population to governmental actions and programs. This last side of the frame is where the

propaganda battle occurs and PPM is the determining factor in victory or defeat. Kitson

also illustrated the crucial link PPM facilitates in the political atmosphere for the

intelligence side of the frame.[55]

Kitson stated the political atmosphere ebbs and flows with the periodic

occurrences of propaganda as PPM is conducted by both sides. Initially, the insurgent has

the advantage in the political atmosphere, Kitson warned. Insurgents initiate their

---

[54]Ibid., 78, 81.

[55]Kitson, *Bunch of Five,* 284-290.

propaganda efforts first and antagonize the population towards the government or governmental policies, putting the government on a defensive and reactive footing. As a result, PPM by the counterinsurgent force is required to highlight the positive attributes of the government more effectively than the insurgents can emphasize the negative attributes of the government, while also discrediting the insurgent organization itself. This requires active monitoring of insurgent propaganda and conducting countering efforts by argumentative and physical means, Kitson wrote. The end result of the battle is the "regaining and retaining"[56] the allegiance of the population in order to ensure the greatest likelihood of acceptance for governmental programs and actions conducted by the coordinating agency, intelligence apparatus, and legal system.[57]

The allegiance factor is especially crucial relative to intelligence gathering, Kitson narrated. In Kitson's frame, intelligence collection is paramount as "the problem of defeating the enemy consists very largely of finding him."[58] Intelligence of the period was largely based on information provided from agents, informers, and information gained from troop contact with the population; what would today be characterized as Human Intelligence (HUMINT). In order to elicit HUMINT from the population, PPM was crucial. In Kitson's words, "All actions designed to retain and regain the allegiance

---

[56]Kitson used the phrase repetitiously throughout *Low Intensity Operations* and *Bunch of Five*.

[57]Kitson, *Bunch of Five*, 286-287.

[58]Kitson, *Low Intensity Operations*, 95.

31

of the population are relevant to the process of collecting background information because its provision is closely geared to the attitude of the people."[59]

Also of interest, in both *Low Intensity Operations* and *Bunch of Five*, Kitson addresses a peculiar form of propaganda rarely recognized: the use of marches and rallies not just as overt opposition a government but also as indirect PPM conducted against security forces. In this peculiar technique, subversives provoke overreactions by security forces and exploit then the overreaction; gaining material for propaganda. In Soviet and Maoist terms, this was called agitation propaganda or agit-prop. The primary aim of an organized march, according to Kitson, is to first to provoke and exploit overreaction and second to influence the government to place restrictions on security forces--decreasing the security forces' ability to perform their mission. Kitson recognized the technique and wrote on the subject not to advocate its use by counterinsurgent PPM forces but as a defensive acknowledgement, in an attempt to preempt insurgent propaganda opportunities.[60]

As illustrated in *Low Intensity Operations* and *Bunch of Five,* Frank Kitson's knowledge and theories contain substantial insight in PPM employment derived from his participation in multiple diverse COIN operations and associated reflection. Kitson contemplated the roles and value of PPM and how it supports his four sided COIN frame. Although nowhere articulated as a set of PPM principles, PPM tenets can be extrapolated from Frank Kitson's collective works and in simplified form are illustrated in figure 3.

---

[59]Ibid., 97.

[60]Kitson, *Bunch of Five*, 293-294.

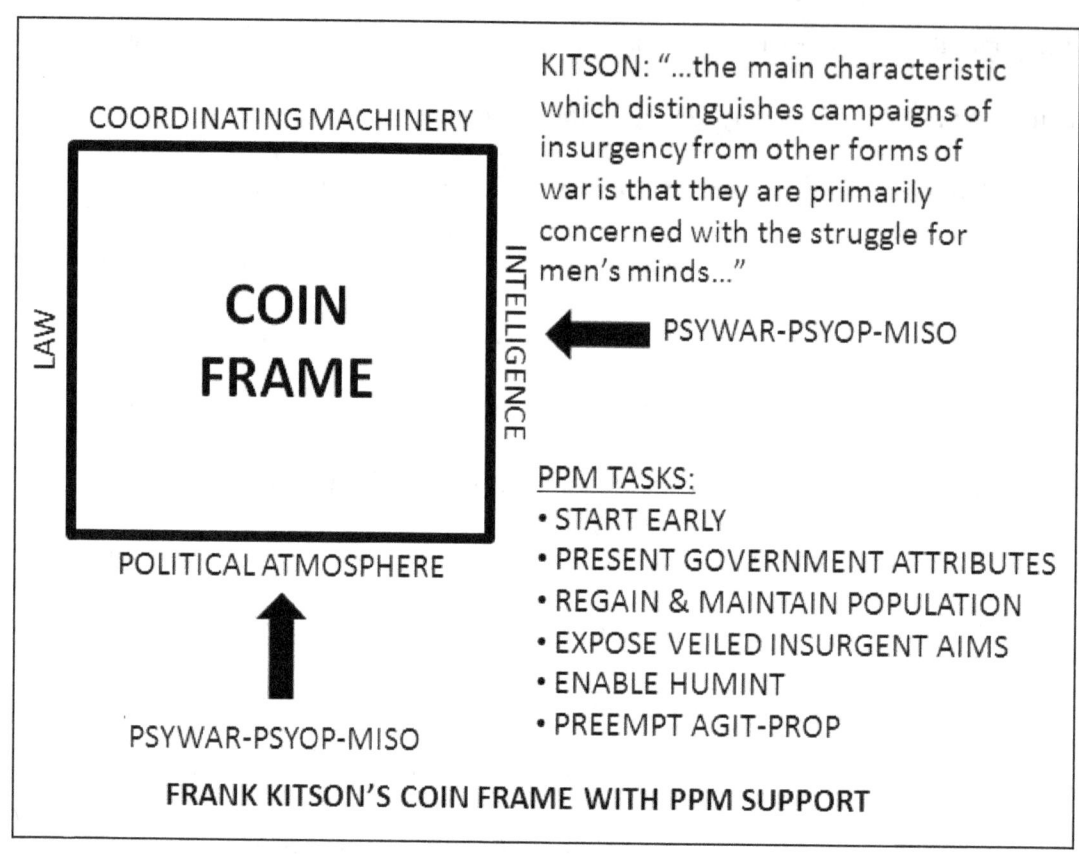

Figure 3.   Frank Kitson's COIN Frame and PPM
Source: Created by author.

<u>Sir Robert Thompson</u>

The contributions of Sir Robert Thompson to modern COIN theory are as unique

as they are authoritative. Thompson's unique perspective stems from his years as a civil

servant. As opposed to his peers, Thompson's experience with insurgencies occurred

while he worked for the British Colonial Civil Service and in civilian advisory capacities.

Although he served in the Royal Air Force with the Chindits in Burma during the Second

World War, the preponderance of his warfare theory was developed while wearing a suit and tie.[61] Serving in a civil capacity, Thompson spent over fifteen consecutive years involved in COIN operations in Malaya and Vietnam.[62] Serving in various capacities, including the Malayan Secretary of Defense and heading the British Advisory Mission (BRIAM) in South Vietnam, Thompson was instrumental in the COIN operations of two conflicts. In fact, during the Vietnam conflict he personally advised the two South Vietnamese Presidents: Ngo Dinh Diem and Nguyen Van Thieu.[63] Later, Thompson also conducted a special assessment of Vietnam for US President Richard Nixon and

---

[61]Thompson entered the Malayan Civil Service in 1938 but joined the Royal Air Force (RAF) in 1941 with the outbreak of the Second World War. Though a trained pilot and an RAF officer, Thompson served in Burma as an air-ground officer, coordinating aerial resupply operations and aerial fire support for the Chindits who conducted harassing attacks behind Japanese lines. After the war, Thompson returned to the civil service. Robert Thompson, *Make for the Hills, Memories of Far Eastern Wars* (London: Leo Cooper Ltd, 1989), 1-32, 41-70.

[62]Post Second World War, Malaya (now Malaysia) remained a British Protectorate until 1957. Three years after the end of expulsion of the Japanese, a communist backed insurgency took place and lasted over a decade. The British assisted the Malayan government in combating the ethnically Chinese insurgents and eventually subdued the movement. In the end, the war known as the Malayan Emergency became one of the few successful counterinsurgencies of the twentieth century. Key to the victory were resettlement operations known as New Villages and paramilitary security forces termed Home Guards; an extensive food rationing operation and curfews were also instrumental. Thompson would later attempt to apply these techniques in Vietnam. See Robert Thompson, *War in Peace, Conventional and Guerrilla Warfare Since 1945* (New York: Harmony Books, 1981).

[63]Ngo Dinh Diem was the President of the Republic of Vietnam (RVN) from 1955 until his assassination in 1963-the founding years of RVN. Nguyen Van Thieu was the president from 1967 to 1975-the final years. Thompson enjoyed a close relationship with both presidents and was instrumental in shaping early Vietnamese pacification policies such as the Strategic Hamlet Program and the Chieu Hoi (Open Arms) amnesty program. Thompson, *Make for the Hills*, 122-130, 158.

continued to advise him periodically.[64] In addition to his experience and relationships, Thompson was also an author.

Characteristic of the foundational counterinsurgency theorists, Thompson captured his vast experiences and theory in writing. Thompson authored a series of works on insurgency consisting of *Defeating Communist Insurgency* in 1966, *No Exit from Vietnam* in 1969, Revolutionary *War in World Strategy* in 1970, and *Peace is Not at Hand* in 1974. Thompson authored, consulted, and edited many other books and articles on twentieth century military history as well. He also published his autobiography, *Make for the Hills*, in 1982, encapsulating his experiences. Of all of Thompson's writings, *Defeating Communist Insurgency* provides the most straight forward articulation of his counterinsurgency theory and reads like an instruction manual in places. Thompson, based on his civil experience, notes in the introduction that the work examines counterinsurgency from more of an administrative viewpoint and less of a military perspective.[65]

In *Defeating Communist Insurgency*, Thompson articulated his strategy for defeating an insurgency in the terms of five principles. He stated the first principle is for a government to have a clear political aim. Creating and nurturing an independent, socially democratic, and united state with economic and political stability lays the foundation for maintaining the citizenry's support, according to Thompson. This aim is broad, he stated, but is essential in attaining or upholding governmental authority. Rule of

---

[64]Thompson, *Make for the Hills*, 158, 161, 165.

[65]Robert Thompson, *Defeating Communist Insurgency* (St. Petersburg, FL: Hailer Publishing, 2005), 10.

Law is Thompson's second principle. Acting outside of established law degrades the legitimacy of the government and degrades its attractiveness, he conveyed. Laws can be strict and oppressive, such as curfews and preemptive detention, but if applied without bias among the entire population, are held as legitimate. Such laws can later be rescinded when conditions permit. Thompson's third principle is the creation of a comprehensive governmental plan for combating an insurgency, not just a military solution but economic, social, and political as well. Balancing and synchronizing civil and military efforts, he states, provides enduring results-combating the insurgents and the causes of insurgency simultaneously. The fourth principle is slightly more complex but closely related to the third. In it, Thompson advocated governmental focus on subversion instead of guerilla or terrorist activity. By combating the political and ideological wing of an insurgent movement, he stated, the insurgent's grasp on the population can be broken. Breaking the grasp isolates the militant insurgents from their required population based support mechanisms such as supplies, intelligence, and secrecy. Thompson's last principle is securing the base areas first. He acknowledged this may cede rural areas to insurgent control but safeguarding the largest population centers and developed regions, provides the government a venue to demonstrate its authority and benefits.[66]

In the framework of these five principles, Thompson incorporated guidelines for the use of PPM. In fact, in *Defeating Communist Insurgency*, he dedicated an entire chapter to what he refers to as Information Services.[67] Inside of Information Services,

---

[66]Ibid., 50-58.

[67]Information Services were an organizational department of British Colonial Civil Administrations. The departments were quasi-PPM and Public Affairs offices

Thompson stated two audiences are to be targeted: psychological warfare is directed at insurgents and information work is directed at the population. Both are to be executed in close coordination with the intelligence organization.[68]

For the insurgents, Thompson prescribed four objectives for psychological warfare: to gain the surrender or defection of insurgents, to create discord between rank-and-file insurgents and their leaders, to create animosity between the insurgents and the population, and to promote positive views of the legitimate government. Thompson elaborated extensively on defection appeals, advocating that combative terms like "surrender" and "prisoner of war" be avoided in favor more palatable suggestions such as offering "safe-conduct" to the "misled." The term "amnesty" should also be avoided, he stated, as it implies a pardon no matter the extent of crimes committed. Rather, a firm but fair appeal articulated succinctly informs the reader that crimes will be punished but justly and legally, acting not only as a surrender appeal but also as a deterrent. Thompson also expanded on dissension. Insurgents' "mistakes and human errors" should be exploited, whether vice or atrocity, to degrade the support of the population and lessen the loyalty of lesser insurgents.[69]

For the population, Thompson offered less of the object of information and more on the method. In a straightforward manner, he conveyed the aim as pulling the population to the government's side and gaining the populations' backing policy. For the

---

which worked on behalf of the supported government. Though civilian in organization, information services generally worked closely with military organizations.

[68] Thompson, *Defeating Communist Insurgency*, 90.

[69] Ibid., 90-95.

method, Thompson stipulated truthfulness and authority as key. Paramount to the legitimacy of the government is credibility, which is maintained by truthful information, according to Thompson. He narrated a failure of truthfulness, in fact or intent, undoes integrity of a hundred other efforts. Likewise, Thompson advised that in order to be respected, an air of authority be present in all governmental propaganda, illustrating dignity and confidence. Taking an apologetic tone, even if mishaps occur, should be avoided. Spinning an unfortunate event, by spotlighting the compensation paid or reconstruction over the collateral damage produces better results he suggests. Noteworthy, Thompson injected a special emphasis relative to "mistakes," stating information services cannot justify mishaps but may defuse a situation with this sleight-of-hand technique. Lastly, Thompson suggested limiting counterpropaganda efforts as engaging in propaganda dialogue draws attention to the insurgents' propaganda. Rather he advises on promoting the government's policy and attributes, forcing the insurgents to counter facts and truth. [70]

Not included in the Information Services chapter but relative to PPM were Thompson's thoughts on rewards systems. Similar to Kitson, Thompson discussed the primacy of intelligence and the role PPM plays in intelligence collection, but from a different angle. Thompson stressed the benefits of effective rewards systems which offered financial incentives for information leading to the capture or killing of insurgents or for the recovery of weapons and war materials. In *Defeating Communist Insurgency*, Thompson summed up the technique stating:

---

[70]Ibid., 90, 96-97.

If there is a well publicized standard rate of rewards for information leading to the killing or capture of terrorists and the recovery of weapons, the natural cupidity of many members of the population soon involves them in the hunt, particularly if they know that their identity will not be revealed and they will be paid on the nail in cash in accordance with the results.[71]

Among the classic counterinsurgents, Thompson provides a viewpoint no other does in that he examined insurgency using governmental rather than military perspectives. Of additionally value, his extensive authorship provided both theoretical and historical dissections of many insurgency campaigns so that patterns could be observed. Also, his views on PPM were direct and supported by his first hand observations of fifteen consecutive years of governmental and military operations. Figure 4 represents a simplified synthesis of Thompson's discussion on PPM application in COIN.

---

[71]Ibid., 88.

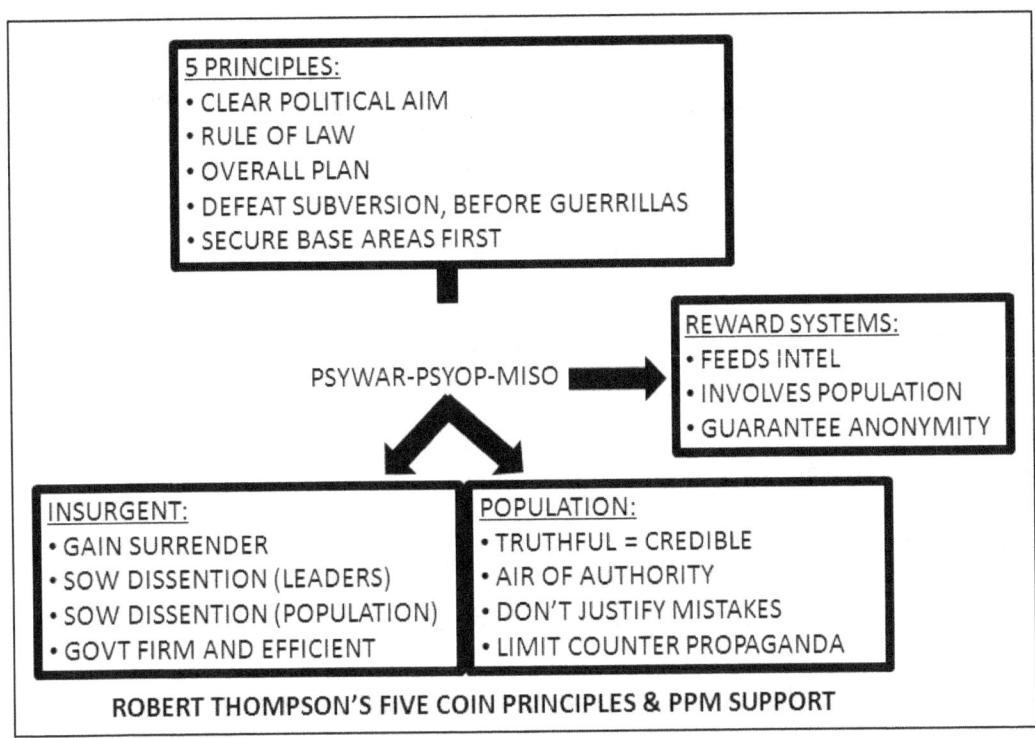

Figure 4.   Robert Thompson's 5 COIN Principles and PPM
Source: Created by author.

David Galula

Lieutenant Colonel David Galula's counterinsurgency theory is considered a key

foundational pillar of current counterinsurgency doctrine. As with his peers, Galula's

writings are born from vast personal experiences; carrying tremendous authority. In 1939

he graduated from Saint Cyr, the French military academy, only months before the

outbreak of the Second World War. After the French capitulation, the collaborating

French Vichy Army dismissed Galula from service, because he was Jewish. So Galula

returned to French Morocco, his previous home, and spied for the Free French until

joining the Free French Army in 1942. With the Free French Army, he saw action in continental Europe, including two amphibious assaults.[72] The conclusion of the war though, fostered Galula's relationship with insurgency as he traveled to China working for the French military attaché from 1945 to 1948. In China, Galula observed firsthand the final years of the Chinese Civil War and Mao Tse-Tung's protracted warfare strategy and associated tactics. Galula was even held captive by the communist guerillas for a short time. Immediately following, while serving in the United Nations Special Commission on the Balkans, Galula observed a second insurgency up close, the Greek civil war. Greek governmental forces defeated the communist insurgents here, with British and American assistance. He also studied the French-Indochina War and the Huk Rebellion, though he did not directly participate, making trips to Indochina and the Philippines while serving as the French military attaché in Hong Kong. Galula's final encounter with insurgency came with the Algerian Revolution, where he commanded a colonial infantry company and applied his observations on counterinsurgency with substantial though localized success. He also served as the deputy battalion commander in Algeria for a short period.[73]

After surviving a world war, multiple insurgencies, and the French political turmoil that followed the Algerian conflict, Galula resigned his commission and sought civilian employment in 1962. During this period, he captured his experiences and theory in two books. The first work, *Pacification in Algeria, 1956-1958*, was written for the RAND Corporation and published in 1963 but remained classified as "confidential" until

---

[72]Ann Marlowe, *David Galula: His Life and Intellectual Context* (Carlisle, PA: Strategic Studies Institute, 2010), 21-45.

[73]David Galula, *Pacification in Algeria* (Santa Monica, CA: RAND Corporation, 1963), 69.

2005. The confidential classification significantly hampered access and proportionately

interest. The second writing, *Counterinsurgency Warfare: Theory and Practice*, was

published in 1964 and though valued in certain military circles, remained relatively

obscure until reemerging as a foundational source for the United States' current

counterinsurgency manual, FM 3-24, *Counterinsurgency*. Though written on the same

subject matter, the two works differ in scope. The former primarily addresses combating

insurgency at a localized level, chronicling Galula's actions in Algeria. The latter is

conceptual, addressing counterinsurgency in a broader sense.[74] Both address the

application of action psychologique, psychological action directed at a population, and

guerre psychologique, psychological warfare directed at insurgents and supporters.[75]

Drawing from his observations and experiences, Galula formulated four

comprehensive counterinsurgency laws. In *Counterinsurgency Warfare: Theory and*

Practice, Galula conveyed the four laws and further articulated eight steps to achieving

success against an insurgency nested in the context of the laws, including aims for PPM.

The first law communicates the population's support is as necessary for the

counterinsurgent as the insurgent. An armed force can drive insurgents from an area, but

the allegiance of a population prevents reemergence and likewise, only with the tacit

support of a population can an insurgency survive. The population, consequently, is the

prize the two forces struggle over, according to Galula. Support is gained through the

active minority is his second stated law. The bulk of populations are relatively

---

[74]Marlowe, *David Galula,* 2-9.

[75]Peter Paret, *French Revolutionary Warfare from Indochina to Algeria, The Analysis of a Political and Military Doctrine* (New York: Frederick A. Praeger, Inc., 1964), 56.

uncommitted during conflicts, no matter the cause, observes Galula. Smaller "active" segments commit to a side and are motivated enough to act. Galula advocates indentifying and influencing receptive active minorities to mobilize the masses, assisted by an acceptable counter-cause. PPM is crucial to this law. In fact, while discussing the law, Galula writes, "the main goal of propaganda [is]-to show that the cause and situation of the counterinsurgent are better than the insurgent's."[76] The third law Galula provided is the population's support is conditional. The pro-government minority remains silent and invisible when physically intimidated by insurgents. Only after localized security is established, can a pro-government minority become an "active" minority. Here, Galula provides another comment on PPM stating "when a man's life is at stake, it takes more than propaganda to budge him." Galula concluded with a fourth law, intensity of efforts and vastness of means is essential. Only concentrated efforts and means provide relief from insurgent control, he argued. Instead of diluting resources across expanses, successive expansion provides the best testament of governmental control.[77]

After describing his four counterinsurgency laws, Galula provided a strategic counterinsurgency formula and scales down the required actions for ground level implementation. The formula consists of eight steps: (1) Destruction or Expulsion of the Insurgent Forces, (2) Deployment of the Static Unit, (3) Contact with and Control of the Population, (4) Destruction of the Insurgent Political Organization, (5) Local Elections, (6) Testing Local Leaders, (7) Organizing a Party, and (8) Winning Over or Suppressing

---

[76]David Galula, *Counterinsurgency Warfare: Theory and Practice* (St. Petersburg: Hailer Publishing, 2005), 77.

[77]Ibid., 74-79.

the Last Guerillas. During the first three of the eight steps, Galula placed a strong

emphasis on PPM. In fact, he allocated almost as much space to the psychological facets

of warfare as he did to the maneuver aspects, in the early steps. He articulated this

emphasis as focusing on three key audiences: counterinsurgent forces, the population,

and the insurgents.[78]

During the first step, destruction or expulsion of the insurgent forces, Galula

directed a select area to be cordoned by mobile forces who conduct an inward sweep

followed by an outward sweep. He pointed out this concentrates insurgent organizations

for destruction and then expels evasive guerrillas. After the operation, a rearguard of the

mobile force controls the area until follow-on static units can be brought in. To capitalize

on the effectiveness of the maneuver operation, Galula directed psychological work on

the three audiences. Collateral damage and disputes with the inhabitants are inherent

consequences of this maneuver, he acknowledged. To diminish the undesired effects,

Galula suggested counterinsurgent forces be indoctrinated with the understanding that

counterinsurgent forces will be held accountable for "misdeeds." Also to preempt

military-population clashes, he advised a neutrality appeal be made to the population.

Galula did not advocate an attempt to garner governmental support from the population

during this step, stating it would be premature and counterproductive. Rather a subtle and

achievable argument should be presented, directing the population not to interfere with

the operation or offer any aid to the insurgents. Lastly, Galula focused on the insurgent.

---

[78]Ibid., 107-135.

In this situation, if an insurgent force chooses to fight instead of flee, it will be destroyed. He concluded that goading the insurgent force to fight then becomes the PPM aim.[79]

Deployment of static forces is the second step. Galula stated that destroying the insurgent force or forcing it to flee does not guarantee it will not reemerge. Follow-on static forces are required to replace the rearguard of the mobile forces, securing the population from new recruits or additional infiltrations, as well as securing civil development administrations. These static forces must be garrisoned among the population, not focused on militarily significant terrain, rather to build common bonds and start garnering the allegiance of the population. To enable this goal, Galula again addressed influencing the three audiences. For the counterinsurgent forces, enemy focused operations will continue but become secondary to population security tasks. Providing the reason behind the shift in tasks to the soldiers, Galula stated, is vital for two reasons. Rationale builds buy-in but also, after hearing the reasoning, leaders can identify soldiers that may not be suited for work with the population-a preemptive measure. For the population, Galula advocates sending the message that the counterinsurgents are here to stay. Presenting this argument sways the population from neutrality to support, gradually. The argument itself is best delivered indirectly, through suggestion for instance long term leasing of housing or lands. Due to the concentration of counterinsurgent forces, Galula advocated continuing the same aim as in step one for the insurgents-provoke them into battle. He suggested an indirect method here as well; delivering dispersion or surrender appeals may trigger the insurgents to fight due to

---

[79]Ibid., 107-110.

pressure exerted on the insurgent leadership. Then the remaining elements can be destroyed.

The third step, contact with and control of the population, is the last step in which Galula provides detailed PPM guidance. This step is perhaps the most critical as it reestablishes authority over the population, isolates the population from the guerrillas, and gathers initial intelligence. Galula conveyed the population will fear insurgent retribution for governmental cooperation. To gain contact then, manufactured scenarios are necessary where counterinsurgent "orders" provide alibis for interaction, like collective work programs. Control is produced through a number of efforts such as identity cards, curfews, travel passes, access control points, etc. These are both reinforced by an increased feel for security, where visible signs of military action continue such as patrols and ambushes. Also, increased security provides a second alibi for the population to not directly support an insurgent group. Additionally, with the increased perception of security and forced contact, informants can be gained, furthering the goals of the step. As for psychological action and warfare during this step, the chief aim for the counterinsurgent forces is influencing soldiers to remain cautious while maintaining friendliness. Galula stated soldiers, once dispersed, will inherently understand safety as function of a positive relationship with the population. Military vigilance must still be reiterated though. Three aims exist for the population. The population needs to be informed why the control measures are in place in order to gain their approval. The gradual work of dissociating the population from the insurgents must start. Conversely, a gradual appeal persuading the neutral to slide to the support of the counterinsurgents must be made. Finally, in the insurgent camp, divide and conquer. A shift in appeal technique is made to address insurgents instead of the insurgent organization. Addressing the group promotes solidarity, addressing the individual encourages dissention.[80] Throughout the following five steps, Galula provides general guidance PPM, not with the detail contained at the onset, though.

Of interest, Galula's first work, the "classified" *Pacification in Algeria*, contains much of the same theory as his second work, the "unclassified" *Counterinsurgency Warfare: Theory and Practice*. The concepts of the active minority, counterinsurgents living amongst the population, and sequential expansion of control are all included in detail in *Pacification in Algeria*. Even the four laws of counterinsurgency are specifically included.[81] Not included in *Counterinsurgency Warfare* though is Galula's discourse on the method to achieve "pacification." He related that during his service in Algeria two schools of thought existed for counterinsurgency and both were equally inadequate. Galula framed the problem from two viewpoints, that of the warriors and that of the psychologists. In his own words, Galula described the former; "At one end stood the 'warriors,' officers who had learned nothing, who challenged the very idea that the population was the real objective, who maintained that military action pursued with sufficient means and vigor for a sufficiently long time would defeat the rebels." He also described the latter; "At the other extreme where the 'psychologists,' most of them recruited among officers who had undergone Vietminh brainwashing in the prison camps. To them, psychological action was the answer to everything."[82] This discourse appears to

---

[80]Ibid., 115-123.

[81]Galula, *Pacification in Algeria*, 246.

[82]Ibid., 64-70.

be the catalyst in which Galula's comprehensive theory was formed: population mobilization gained by balancing military action and psychological action.

Galula, equally as experienced as the other classic counterinsurgents, holds a special position in that his writings on COIN theory and PPM application are comprehensive yet incredibly detailed. In his writings he provided the overarching purpose of PPM as affirming the "cause and situation" of the government superior to that of the insurgents. Uniquely though, Galula also systematically addresses the application of PPM through the tactical progression of his eight step operation. In fact, he devoted as much consideration to PPM as maneuver operations in the first three steps. Lastly, all of the classic counterinsurgents address a balanced approach in COIN, however, only Galula addresses in detail the two extreme ends of the argument between the "warriors" and the "psychologists." A condensed summary of Galula's COIN theory and application is provided in figure 5.

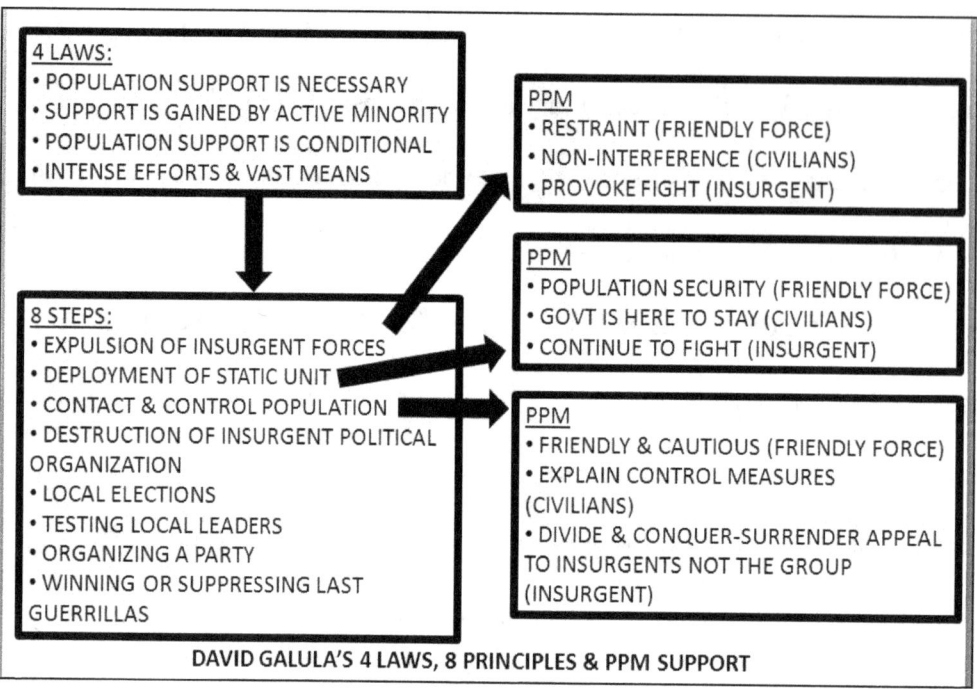

Figure 5.   David Galula's 4 Laws, 8 Steps, and PPM
Source: Created by author.

Major General Edward Lansdale

Major General Edward Lansdale is the United States' long forgotten Cold War counterinsurgency expert. Lansdale combated insurgencies and revolutionary movements from the Philippines to Cuba, serving in various capacities from the Second World War through the Vietnam War. Recruited into the Office of Strategic Services (OSS) in 1943 and simultaneously working in the Army Military Intelligence Service (MIS), he spent most of the Second World War stateside performing intelligence, counterintelligence, and "handyman" work.[83] After the war and through the early 1950s, Lansdale served

---

[83]Cecil B. Currey, *Edward Lansdale, The Unquiet American* (Boston: Houghton Mifflin Company, 1988), 18-25; Jonathon Nashel, *Edward Lansdales's Cold War* (Boston: University of Massachusetts Press, 2005), 29.

extensively in the Philippines as an Army officer and an Air Force officer but primarily

as a Central Intelligence Agency (CIA) agent.[84] After years of Japanese domination and

following Philippine independence in 1946, the nation experienced a communist backed

insurgency known as the Huk Rebellion.[85] With the assistance of the Joint U.S. Military

Advisory Group (JUSMAG) and Lansdale's advice on civic action and psychological

warfare, the rebellion was quelled.[86] Due to his success, Lansdale was dispatched to

Indochina in 1954 to assist the interim South Vietnamese government and to ensure US

interests were maintained and to avoid an eventual communist takeover.[87] More

specifically, he was to "weaken the newly formed northern government of Ho Chi Minh

through whatever means possible and to strengthen the government of the southern

---

[84]Lansdale held a commission in the US Army and the US Air Force but at some point in the early 1950s became a field operative for the CIA. He never attended flight training and never held an Air Force command yet became a Major General before retiring from the Air Force in 1963. See Nashel, 77.

[85]The Hukbalahap Rebellion, commonly called the Huk Rebellion, was a post Second World War communist insurrection in the Philippines. The Huk Rebellion lasted almost a decade, 1946 to 1954, and was partially a carry-over from the Japanese occupation of the Philippines. The *Hukbong Bayan Laban sa Hapon* [People's Anti-Japanese Army] was formed during the early 1940s and was guided by the *Partido Komunista ng Pilipinas* [Philippine Communist Party]. After the Japanese were driven from the islands by US forces and Filippino guerrillas, the Huks continued to fight but against the western oriented Filippino government. Through a series political, social, economic, and military actions taken by the Phillipino government, the rebellion was quelled. The conflict was of strategic interest to the United States as after Philippine independence, many US military bases and ports remained.

[86]Nashel, 31-48.

[87]The French Indochina war ended in 1954 with the Geneva Peace Accords stipulating the Vietnam be divided into two provisional states. The southern state became the western backed Republic of Vietnam (RVN) and the communist backed northern state became the Democratic Republic of Vietnam (DRV). The accords stipulated the two provisional states hold centralized elections in 1956 to reunite the country.

regions headed by Ngo Dinh Diem."[88] In South and North Vietnam, Lansdale heavily influenced the political and military landscape and worked extensively on national building efforts in the south. Departing in 1956, he returned periodically to assess and advise, and in 1960 drafted the US counterinsurgency support plan for South Vietnam.[89] He returned again in 1965 and served in various advisory roles through 1968. In between his time in Vietnam, Lansdale was also involved in other irregular warfare initiatives and served as the executive officer of the Special Group-Augmented (SGA) which planned Operation MONGOOSE-the subversive overthrow of Cuba.[90]

Lansdale, as a COIN practitioner and theorist, conveyed his theories on COIN differently than did Kitson, Thompson, and Galula. In his one published book, *In the Midst of Wars: An American's Mission to Southeast Asia,* Lansdale communicated his theories on COIN but in a historical narrative rather than a theoretical model. In it, he discussed his views and actions to defeat insurgency in the Philippines and somewhat in early South Vietnam. The work did not include commentary on his Vietnam experience

---

[88]Edward G. Lansdale, *In the Midst of Wars: An American's Mission to Southeast Asia* (New York: Harper and Row Publishers, 1972), xi.

[89]In 1961 Lansdale submitted a Vietnamese counterinsurgency support plan to the Kennedy administration for that included a substantial increase in aid in order to slightly increase the size of the Vietnamese armed forces but double the size of the Vietnamese paramilitary forces-the Civil Guard. He recommended the situation receive "emergency treatment" and the "best people" to advise and assist. See Robert S. McNamara, James G. Blight, and Robert K. Brigham. *Argument Without End: In Search of Answers to the Vietnam Tragedy* (New York: PublicAffairs, 1999), 323.

[90]The SGA was a special advisory group for the Kennedy administration. Operation Mongoose was never executed but was later the subject of much controversy as it included "executive actions," such as the assassination of Cuba's President Fidel Castro and the poisoning of food crops.

of the late 1960s though. Also, the work contained no list of principles or framework for counterinsurgency operations; they have to be extrapolated out of the account.[91]

The type of COIN operation Lansdale advocated was holistic in nature including social, political, economic, military, and psychological efforts. Primarily, he understood insurgency and counterinsurgency as a people's war dealing with "real live human beings out there."[92] Due to these inclinations, Lansdale weighted the facets of counterinsurgency with political and psychological tenets having primacy but supported by military and economic efforts.[93] He communicated this primacy as using the euphemism of the "x-factor." The x-factor was simply how people felt about their conditions, movement, war, etc. Lansdale saw the x-factor as the crucial difference between conventional warfare and irregular warfare such as insurgency and counterinsurgency.[94]

Lansdale's concept for COIN was best illustrated in the Philippines, where as an advisor, he brought his understandings to full manifestation. There he addressed the

---

[91]Apart from the PPM concepts conveyed in Lansdale's' *In the Midst of Wars*, Lansdale presented several lectures where he articulated his thoughts on PPM. Since *In the Midst of Wars* includes no specified formula or theory for PPM application in COIN, the transcripts from two of his lectures are included in this thesis to reinforce the author's extrapolated opinion of Lansdale's PPM theory. These transcripts are Appendix C and Appendix D of this thesis and are from a lecture series given in 1960 to the Armed Forces Staff College in Norfolk, Virginia. The transcripts recount many of the same incidents found in *In the Midst of Wars*, and also emphasize Lansdale's view of PPM as a weapon system much like artillery. See Edward Geary Lansdale Collection, Box 80, Folder: Military Psychological Operations and Military Psychological Operations: Part Two, Hoover Institution Archives.

[92]Currey, 307.

[93]Ibid., 279.

[94]Rufus Phillips, *Why Vietnam Matters: An Eyewitness Account of Lessons Not Learned* (Annapolis, MD: Naval Institute Press, 2008), xiii, xiv, 312.

social and political concerns of the rural Filippinos and dealt with the insurgents. To deal with the sociological and economic conditions of the Filippinos, Lansdale influenced judicial reform by making military Judge Advocate lawyers available for peasants to settle land disputes. To provide the people with a political voice, he opened direct communications between the peasants and the government by implementing the ten-centavo telegram. To deal with the insurgents, Lansdale and his team spearheaded Philippine Scout Rangers who conducted small scale counterguerrilla operations. Also, he offered the insurgents a chance to defect and reintegrate into society. With his help, the Economic Development Corps (EDC) was expanded and provided surrendered Huks the opportunity to receive vocational training and land grants. His philosophy on amnesty programs was simply "why shoot a man if you could talk him into surrendering."[95] Other efforts were also created yet these illustrate Lansdale's approach.[96]

More heavily any other prominent counterinsurgent practitioner-theorist though, Lansdale focused on PPM. This aspect of Lansdale is likely due to his civilian years, where is worked as a journalist and advertising executive.[97] In PPM, Lansdale took a two-prong approach, one geared at building support for the government and one aimed at disrupting enemy efforts. To build support for the government, the Civil Affairs Office (CAO) was created. Recognizing that the army was the face of the government to most Filippinos, the CAO set out to "sell" the army to the people. The CAO was the enabler not the agent; it manifested a small section attached to each army brigade with the task of

---

[95]Nashel, 129.

[96]Lansdale, 48-59.

[97]Nashel, 25-26.

training Soldiers to be "brothers and protectors of the population." The CAO also encouraged military participation in civil events and the construction of public works. Although some resistance was encountered to the "non-military" work, Lansdale provided practical incentives as:

> Troop commanders were not always willing to undertake civic action with their soldiers because they viewed this action as "political" and therefore outside their military domain. To persuade them to try it, I pointed out that one reward of brotherhood was the willingness of the people to talk more openly with the soldiers. If a commander were to practice civic action honestly and thoroughly, I guaranteed that it would increase his unit's "raw take" of tactical intelligence by 100 percent in a week. It often took less time than that. [98]

For disrupting the enemy, Lansdale was an incredibly creative thinker and focused PSYWAR in the most irregular methods. Though he used mass media and technology, he favored face to face communications in persuasion and innuendo. In particular he remarked, "The Asia people know that the mouth and the ear were invented long before the printing press, the camera, and the radio," illustrating his insight.[99] He summed up his philosophy as:

> Conventional military men think of combat psywar almost exclusively in term of leaflets or broadcasts appealing to the enemy to surrender. Early on, I realized that psywar had a wider potential to than that. A whole new approach opened up, for example, when one thinks of psywar in terms of playing a practical joke.[100]

Many of Lansdale's "practical jokes" would be illegal in the contemporary environment and were likely illegal then. Taken in context though, two general principles can be derived from them.

---

[98]Lansdale, 70-71.

[99]Ibid., 42.

[100]Ibid., 71.

The first principle could be termed Shepherding. Inside of a counterinsurgency fight, friendly and enemy population groups can be persuaded, coerced, or otherwise induced to move to or from a location for tactical or strategic gains of the counterinsurgent force.[101] On several occasions, Lansdale and his subordinates used irregular psychological methods to stimulate groups to move into or out of an area. One of the tactical examples was the vampire incident. At one point during the Huk Rebellion, a Huk guerrilla force had occupied a particular hill next to a village where a Philippine army force was garrisoned. The army needed to be relocated due to operational requirements but could not leave the village to the will of the Huks nor was the garrison strong enough to push the Huks out. A PPM solution was developed. Based on the Filippino's superstitious beliefs, a "PSYWAR team" introduced the notion that a vampire was in the area. The PSYWAR team planted rumors in the village of vampire sightings, knowing Huk sympathizers would communicate the rumor to the Huk guerrillas. After sufficient time passed for the rumor to circulate, the team "silently snatched" a member of a Huk patrol, drained his blood, marked his neck with two puncture wounds, and put his body back on a commonly used trail. After the Huks discovered the body the following day, the entire squadron left the hill, according to Lansdale.[102]

One strategic example of shepherding was the Catholic migration. In late 1954 and early 1955, approximately 900,000 Catholic Vietnamese living in northern Vietnam

---

[101]The "principles" are not listed as such in Lansdale's writings. The principles are derived from Lansdale's historical account and listed as principles for ease of explanation.

[102]Other examples of induced movements are provided. See Lansdale, 72-73; Nashel, 40-41.

migrated or were evacuated to southern Vietnam.[103] The added Catholic population was a

benefit to the western friendly and Catholic South Vietnamese leader, Ngo Dinh Diem,

who became president in 1955. Obviously, Lansdale's PSYWAR operations did not

trigger the migration; a number of circumstances stimulated the movement such as fear of

reprisals against the Franco-friendly Catholics. Lansdale did develop it though.

Disseminating leaflets showing concentric circles over Hanoi, suggesting a US atomic

strike; spreading rumors of Chinese military aggression in northern Vietnam; and selling

thousands of pseudo-almanac predicting dire times for northern Vietnam; Lansdale

exploited existing tension to amplify the effects.[104]

The second principle could be termed Boomerang Propaganda. If effectively

studied and authentically replicated, insurgent propaganda can be used to counter the

insurgent's causes and operations. On multiple occasions Lansdale used this technique

for great effect. One example was the Boycott the Election. During the 1951 Philippine

presidential election, Lansdale used one of the Huk's slogans against them--"bullets not

ballots." Lansdale had received reports of a Huk agit-prop cell working in Manila.[105]

Through proxies, Lansdale presented a pseudo-directive to the agit-prop cell with the

---

[103]Lansdale, 167.

[104]Robert D. Schulzinger, *A Time for War: The United States and Vietnam, 1941-1975* (Oxford: Oxford University Press, 1997); Lansdale, 226; Phillips, 39-40; Nashel, 60-61; Pentagon Papers Volume 1, 579.

[105]Agit-prop is an acronym for agitation and propaganda. Agitprop is a standard technique doctrinally employed by Marxist-Leninist movements and the "peoples" movements that have followed. The aim of agitprop is two-fold. First, is to encourage and control seditious acts such as labor strikes, protests, and riots. Second, is to cause governmental or interventionist forces to over react to the seditious act for the purpose of further propaganda exploitation.

slogan "Boycott the Election."[106] Being in line with existing precedent, the agit-prop cell used the slogan in their propaganda efforts and effectively encouraged Huks not to vote. Though maybe counter to a political-inclusion narrative for counterinsurgency, the act did assist in assuring in assuring a pro-western government was elected and had a demoralized effect of the Huks, according to Lansdale.[107]

Another example of boomerang propaganda was executed by one of Lansdale's subordinates, Rufus Phillips. This incident, Dongs for Piasters, utilized the agit-prop notion as well. In early 1955, the division between South Vietnam and North Vietnam was in process. Due to the establishment of the two peer governments and the banking industry being largely controlled by the French, the value of the South Vietnamese piaster was influx. During the period, the Viet Minh had also established a currency, the dong. At some areas, the value of the dong greatly outweighed the value of the piaster. To exploit this condition and incite anti-Viet Minh sentiment, Phillips used Lansdale's technique to produce a Viet Minh pseudo-leaflet offering to exchange dongs or piasters on a one for one basis.[108] After being disseminated, the pseudo-leaflet did incite a riot of angry labors who could not exchange their piasters as promised, eroding credibility and support for the Viet Minh.[109]

---

[106]For authenticity, the pseudo-directive was typed on a captured Huk typewriter, used captured Huk paper, and included secret Huk authenticating identification.

[107]Lansdale, 92-93.

[108]The Viet Minh pseudo-leaflet was not hastily prepared but was a product of detailed intelligence and analysis. Former Viet Minh proclamations, paper, type face, and writing style were all analyzed to recreate credible reproductions. Phillips, 68.

[109]Phillips, 67-69.

General Lansdale, in the case of the Philippines, was one of few counterinsurgents to be successful in the twentieth century. Lansdale's emphasis on a holistic approach, heavily weighted with civic and psychological aspects, proved effective when correctly applied. Although many of his methods may have appeared "unsound"; his pragmatic and innovative techniques did deliver the cumulative desired effect. Yet a true difficulty arises in evaluating his concepts. The difficulty lays in his intrinsically covert nature and in understanding his *In the Midst of Wars,* though written as a historical account, arguably contains a few "white lies."[110] An extrapolated and condensed interpretation of Lansdale's views on PPM is illustrated in figure 6.

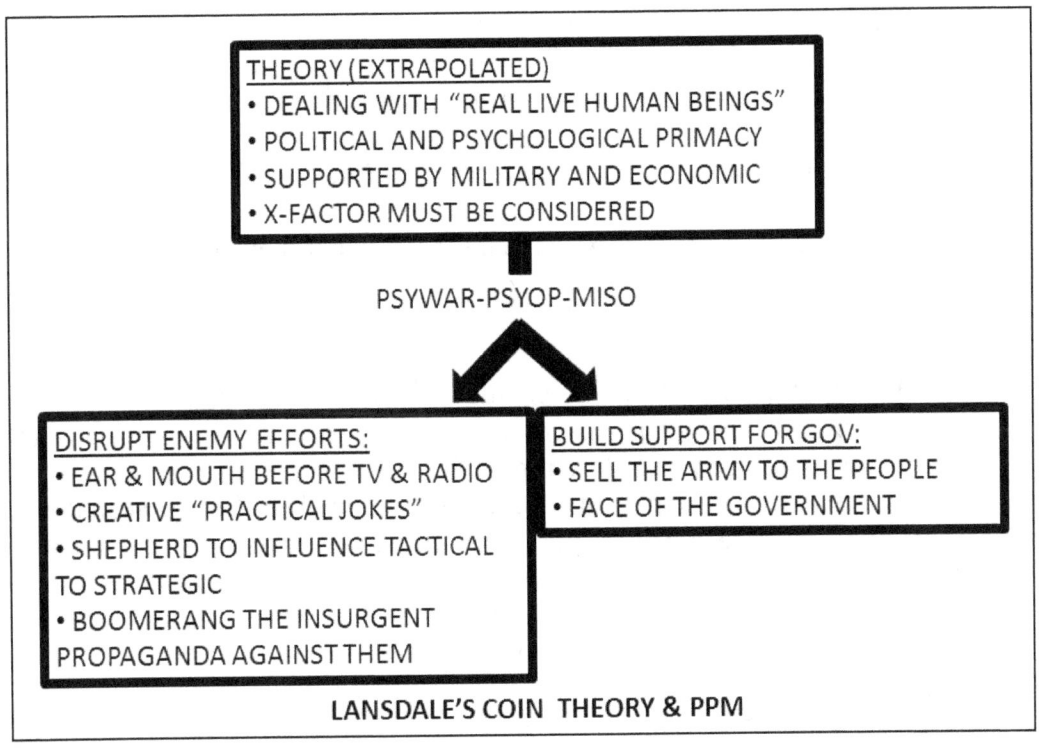

Figure 6.   Lansdale's COIN Theory and PPM
Source: Created by author.

---

[110]Currey, 329.

Classic Counterinsurgent PPM Synthesis

Synthesizing the cumulative PPM experience of the four classic counterinsurgents, Frank Kitson, Robert Thompson, David Galula, and Edward Lansdale; is no easy task as they each conveyed their ideas in different manners. To add to the complexity, it must be acknowledged that each classic counterinsurgent's works undoubtedly possess some degree of ego, self interest, and interpretation. However, aims, principles, and in some cases tactics; can be pulled from each practitioner-theorist's writing. If patterns can be identified in their works, they may be more useful than doctrine as consistency found among four separate expert opinions, each compiled independently, is more valid than conglomerate opinion expressed in doctrine.

First, did the classic counterinsurgents agree on the primary aim of PPM in supporting COIN? Though phrased in many different expressions, all four of the classic counter insurgents comment that the primary purpose of PPM in COIN is to induce the population to support the government over the insurgent. This is evidenced in their own words:

> Frank Kitson: "There has never been much doubt that the main characteristic which distinguishes campaigns of insurgency from other forms of war is that they are primarily concerned with the struggle for men's minds, since only by succeeding in such a struggle with a large enough number of people can the rule of law be undermined and constitutional institutions be overthrown. Violence may play a greater or lesser part in the campaign, but it should be used very largely in support of ideas. In a conventional war the reverse ifs more usually the case and propaganda is normally deployed in support of armed might."[111]

> Robert Thompson: "the task naturally falls into two categories: information work directed at the insurgents (i.e. psychological warfare) and information work directed at the public. Not only do the two go together, but the first requires very close co-operation with the intelligence organization. The aim of the first is to

---

[111]Kitson, *Bunch of Five*, 282.

reduce the will of the insurgents to fight and to encourage surrenders, while the aim of the second is to rally the population to the side of the government and to encourage positive support for the government in its campaign."[112]

David Galula: "This truism dictates the main goal of propaganda-to show that the cause and the situation of the counterinsurgent are better than the insurgent's."[113]

Edward Lansdale. "Essentially, in a revolutionary 'people's war,' the people of the country actually constitute the true battleground of the war. Whoever wins them wins the war."

Second, did the classic counterinsurgents agree common principles or tactics for PPM in COIN? This answer is much more difficult to arrive at but some key principles do resonate among the works. For the purpose of this synthesis, if two of the four classic counterinsurgents mentioned the principle or tactic in their independent works, it is considered noteworthy. Though not all inclusive and subject to some interpretation, agreed upon principles included:

1. PPM amnesty/reconciliation programs (4 mentioned.) All of the classics discussed amnesty programs. Though PPM organizations do not administer the programs, PPM is key in the process. Of note, three of four discussed the significance of the jargon of "return" or "rally" instead of "surrender." Thompson and Lansdale discussed the tactic in greater detail; both had observed first hand successes with the tactic in Malaya and the Philippines.[114]

2. PPM requires Propaganda of the Deed (3 mentioned). Kitson, Thompson, and Lansdale all addressed a necessity for "propaganda of the deed" though they

---

[112]Thompson, *Defeating Communist Insurgency*, 90.

[113]Galula, *Counterinsurgency Warfare*, 77.

[114]Kitson, *Bunch of Five*, 146-148; Thompson, *Defeating Communist Insurgency*, 90-92; Galula, *Pacification in Algeria*, 225; Lansdale, 48, 129.

did not all use the term, stating PPM must be supported by tangible improvement or supportable facts such as land grants, a functional reconciliation program, or the establishment of security.[115]

3. <u>PPM enables HUMINT (3 mentioned)</u>. Kitson, Thompson, and Lansdale, all include specific statements in their works indicating that PPM is vital to enabling and exploiting HUMINT. The principle is suggested in Galula's *Pacification in Algeria* but not explicitly stated.[116]

4. <u>PPM must preempt agit-prop (2 mentioned)</u>. Kitson and Lansdale both warned of insurgents inciting riots in order to provoke security forces and create opportunities for propaganda.[117]

5. <u>PPM must uncover Veiled Aims (2 mentioned)</u>. Kitson and Thompson discussed identifying and making known the veiled aims of insurgents such as the Indochinese Communist party promoting nationalism instead of communism.[118]

---

[115]Kitson, *Low Intensity Operations*, 79; Thompson, *Defeating Communist Insurgency*, 92, 96; *Lansdale*, 48, 70-71.

[116]Kitson, *Low Intensity Operations*, 97, 189; Thompson, *Defeating Communist Insurgency*, 88; Galula, *Pacification in Algeria*, 230, 276, 288; Lansdale, 71.

[117]Kitson, *Low Intensity Operations*, 41, 85; Kitson, *Bunch of Five*, 293-294; Lansdale, 71.

[118]Kitson, *Low Intensity Operations*, 30, 85; Thompson, *Defeating Communist Insurgency*, 23.

6. <u>PPM by civilian agencies may be more effective. (2 mentioned.)</u> Kitson and

Thompson both discussed advocacy for civilian led PPM. Both caveated

civilian organizations require military support during COIN operations.[119]

These four men, Frank Kitson, Robert Thompson, David Galula, and Edward

Lansdale; all practiced and observed PPM in multiple COIN operations and each enjoyed

a different perspective. Some valued PPM more and a few less; some were creative and

others traditional in their approach to PPM application; each though considered PPM an

essential and integral part of a comprehensive COIN campaign. Since each reflected and

wrote separately, no consensus was required; but some patterns were observed. The

following two case studies are evaluated against this derived synthesis. Reduced to its

simplest terms, the synthesis of the PPM theories of the four classic counterinsurgents are

illustrated in figure 7.

CLASSIC COUNTERINSURGENT PPM SYNTHESIS

ACCORDING TO ALL FOUR CLASSIC COUNTERINSURGENTS, THE PRIMARY AIM OF COIN PPM IS TO SWAY THE POPULATION TO SUPPORT THE GOVERNMENT OVER THE INSURGENT.

AGREED UPON PRINCIPLES INCLUDE:
• AMNESTY / RECONCILIATION EFFORTS ARE KEY
• PPM REQUIRES PROPAGANDA OF DEED TO BE CREDIBLE
• PPM ENABLES HUMINT
• PPM MUST PREEMPT AGIT-PROP
• PPM MUST UNCOVER VEILED AIMS OF INSURGENTS
• PPM MAY BE RUN CIVILIAN AGENCIES IF AUGMENTED BY MILITARY

Figure 7.   Synthesis of Classic Counterinsurgent PPM theories
Source: Created by author.

---

[119]Kitson, *Low Intensity Operations*, 79, 188; Thompson, *Defeating Communist Insurgency*, 95.

The following chapters include two case studies of how PPM was applied in two separate COIN conflicts. Each illustrates the essentialness of effective PPM in COIN operations. Both case studies also provide a number of best practices for COIN PPM.

CHAPTER 4

COIN PPM OF THE DHOFAR REBELLION

Persuading a man to join you is far cheaper than killing him. Words are far, far less expensive than bullets, let alone shells and bombs. Then, too, by killing him you merely deprive the enemy of one soldier. If he is persuaded to join the Government forces the enemy again become one less, but the Government forces become one more, a gain of plus two.
— Major General Tony Jeapes, *SAS Secret War*

Context of the Conflict

At the height of the Cold War, a relatively unknown though strategically significant war occurred along the southern Arabian peninsula. While the western world focused on the highly visible conflicts in Vietnam and Israel, a gradual and discreet struggle occurred -the prize for which was access to the Middle East's oil reserves. As the free world pondered the domino theory in Southeast Asia, the communist world pondered a similar theory for the Middle East where the western world's oil supply could be interdicted by controlling just two countries, present day Yemen and Oman. Chokepoints to the major oil shipping lanes exist geographically where the Persian Gulf opens to the Arabian Sea (Strait of Hormuz), skirting Oman, and again where the Arabian Sea necks down into the Red Sea and eventually the Suez Canal (Bad El-Mandab), along Yemen's coast (see figure 8). If these strategic bottlenecks fell under the sway of the communist world the political dynamics of the world could be irrevocably changed due to the western economies dependency on Middle Eastern oil.[120]

---

[120]Roger Cole and Richard Belfied, *SAS: Operation Storm* (London: Hodder and Stoughton Ltd. 2011), 17-22.

Compounding the problem was the wide transition from colonial government systems established by the empires of the previous century. As a continuing result of the Second World War and a number of "small wars" that followed, socio-political paradigms were shifting in the United Kingdom -resulting in a gradual reduction of the empire's global footprint. Western reduction left many developing countries open to exploitation by communist movements, among them Yemen[121] and Oman. Both states were British protectorates for most of the twentieth century, with trade and protection agreements dating back to as early as 1646.[122] Policy shifts though called for a gradual reduction in British forces abroad, shrinking the envelope of protection that could be offered.

Yemen was the first to fall. With the withdrawal of British forces in 1967, after several years of civil war and insurgency, communist revolutionaries took control of the region. Afterwards, the conglomerate nation became the People's Democratic Republic of Yemen (PDRY) and was supported politically and economically by the Peoples Republic of China (PRC), the Democratic Peoples Republic of Korea (DPRK), the Republic of Cuba (Cuba), and the Union of Soviet Socialist Republics (USSR).[123] Once established on the peninsula, the revolutionary movement quickly spread to Oman.

The Omani region that bordered PDRY was and is known as Dhofar, and Dhofar was ripe for communist exploitation. Dhofar, in the mid-1960s, was already in a state of rebellion against the Sultanate of Oman. Additionally, an earlier rebellion had been

---

[121]"Yemen" is a loose term referencing a region more so than a nation. Yemen experienced multiple name changes, confederations, political orientations, and border arrangements during the mid-twentieth century relative to shifting alliances of local sheikhdoms and emirates. The region or areas in the region have also been known as Aden, North and South Yemen, the Federation of South Arabia, and the People's Democratic Republic of Yemen. Different segments of the region were also viewed in varying manners by the western world, for instance Aden was a British crown colony from 1936 to 1967 whereas South Yemen was a British protectorate during the same period. Aden's seaport made it strategically valuable while most of the peripheral states held little military, political, or economic importance.

[122]Rowland White, *Storm Front* (London: Bantam Press, 2011), 17-18.

[123]Ibid., 18.

defeated in the previous decade-with help from the British. The existing rebellion, started in 1965, was led by the Dhofar Liberation Front (DLF). The rebellion was quickly usurped by the communist movement from PDRY and reflagged as a movement of the Popular Front for the Liberation of the Occupied Arabian Gulf (PFLOAG).[124] PFLOAG, using the proven Maoist tactics of coercion and indoctrination, rapidly gained control over the rural region except for a few governmental enclaves along the coast where guerilla tactics could not overcome massed firepower, namely Salalah where the Sultan of Oman resided (see figure 9).[125]

---

[124]Popular Front for the Liberation of the Occupied Arabian Gulf (PFLOAG) changed its name to the Popular Front for the Liberation of Oman and the Arabian Gulf in 1972 and to the Popular Front for the Liberation of Oman (PFLO) in 1974. Additionally, PFLOAG absorbed the National Democratic Front for the Liberation of the Occupied Arabian Gulf (NDFLOAG), a related communist movement in northern Oman, early in the conflict. At its height, PFLOAG was estimated to have controlled 2,000 guerrilla fighters and 3,000 auxiliary fighters. By 1975, PFLOAG numbers were estimated at approximately 400 guerrilla fighters and 400 auxiliaries.

[125]Tony Jeapes, *SAS Secret War, Operation Storm in the Middle East* (London: Green Hill Books, 2005), 25-26.

Apart from the communist provocation, a number of circumstances led to the

rebellion. First, the ethnic majority of Dhofar, known as Dhofaris or Jebelis, were an

ethnic and linguistic minority in Oman.[126] The Dhofaris were similar in appearance and

custom to North Africans, such as Ethiopians and Somalis, more so than peninsula Arabs.

As often occurs in polyglots and multi-ethnic societies, an ethnic tension existed. Here it

was between the Dhofaris and the Arabs. Also, Dhofaris were semi-nomadic herdsmen

who pastured goat, cattle, and camel herds in the mountainous areas of Oman. In the

highlands, the Dhofaris felt few ties to the Arabs of the coastal plains of Muscat and

---

[126]"Jebel" is the Arabic word for "mountain." "Jebelis" is a colloquial term for
"Dhofaris" meaning "mountain people" similar in connotation to Vietnamese
"Montagnards" or Scottish "Highlanders."

Salalah.[127] As of the late 1960s, Said Bin Taimur Al Busaidi, the Sultan of Oman, had done little in the way of civil development for the country. Ruling for almost forty years, the Sultan firmly held all authority in the country as an absolute monarchy. He restricted travel, education, and medical services. Though heavily reliant on the British, Said Bin Taimur was vehemently anti-western and viewed "modern" practices as anti-Islamic. Even after the oil revenues of the late 1960s dramatically changed the economic standing of Oman, the Sultan refused to develop the country.[128]

As a result of communist subversion and support coupled with Omani governmental shortcomings, from 1965 to 1970, the Dhofar rebellion was fought with limited success by the Sultan's Armed Forces (SAF). SAF commanded and staffed by British seconded officers and British contract officers, possessed a wealth of combat experienced leaders. Likewise, with most of the soldiers coming from Pakistani Baluchistan or northern Oman, the fighting forces were tough and martial.[129] Although the SAF were effective at counter guerrilla tactics in the countryside and static defenses of the enclave cities, the flow of arms and political inspiration continued coming from across the PDRY border. In order to prevent Oman from becoming a second South Arabian communist proxy state and safeguard Persian Gulf oil trade routes, the United Kingdom intervened, although in a very discreet manner; a coup.

---

[127]Brian Ray, Dangerous *Frontiers, Campaigning in Somaliland & Oman* (Barnsley, South Yorkshire: Pen and Sword Books Ltd., 2008), 60.

[128]White, *Storm Front*, 23.

[129]John Akehurst, *We Won A War, The Campaign in Oman 1965-1975* (Wiltshire Great Britain: Michael Russell Publishing Ltd., 1982), 33-35.

Some details remain clouded but the only son of Sultan Said Bin Taimur, Qaboos, overthrew his father in a coup in 1970. The coup received the backing and support of the British government and the dynamics of the Dhofar rebellion subsequentially changed. Qaboos was western educated and a graduate of the British military academy at Sandhurst. Also, he had previously served in the British army in Germany for a brief time. His experiences abroad led him to a fundamentally different understanding of government than his father had held and he opened the country to civil and economic development. Additionally, Qaboos requested the assistance of other nations in combating the communist insurgency and empowered the SAF with equipment, capabilities, and partners to defeat the insurgency.[130]

Framework of the Counterinsurgency, 1970 to 1975

Over the next five years, a comprehensive counterinsurgency operation was conducted which resulted in the eventual defeat of the PLFOAG insurgency. Numerous factors and circumstances contributed to the victory, some organizational, some governmental, some diplomatic, and some strictly military. Combined, these factors had a choking effect on the insurgency, and with time and intensity eventually strangled the enemy lines of communication (LOCs), recruiting efforts, and political viability.

The first of the initiatives that contributed to the defeat of the PFLOAG was the introduction of British Special Air Service (SAS) personnel, known as the British Army Training Team (BATT) while in Oman. Though originally deployed to Oman as the personal security element for the new Sultan, the role of the SAS quickly grew in

---

[130]Ian Gardiner, *In the Service of the Sultan* (Barnsley, South Yorkshire: Pen and Sword Books Ltd., 2006), 24-25.

particularly as the developer of indigenous security forces. The SAS developed the idea of "turning" the insurgent guerrilla bands to support the Sultan's government instead of the communists. Over the period of just a year, the SAS developed five groups of security forces known as firquats, literally "teams" in Arabic.[131] Through a combination of military action and persuasion, the SAS recruited, trained, and led several firquats of local Dhofaris in combat action against the communist insurgents known as the *adoo*.[132] The program was primarily based on offering Surrendered Enemy Personnel (SEPs) the opportunity to earn an income in the service of the Sultan. By finding a "coincidence of aims," the SAS were able to exploit the existing capabilities of the indigenous fighters against the communist backed insurgency.[133]

The introduction of the SAS though was only part of the solution. Starting in 1970, SAF itself transformed and expanded. Starting out with only two infantry battalions and some associated support, the size of the force increased several fold over the course of two years- greatly expanding its capabilities and reach. Quantities and qualities of armaments also increased as the force was modernized; jets, helicopters, and naval vessels were either added or upgraded. Also SAF was augmented with Royal Air Force

---

[131] The original five Firquats were all recruited, trained, and led by the SAS or 'BATT.' These Firquats consisted of the Firquat Salahadin (FS), Firquat Khalid bin Waleed (FKW), Firquat Azifat (FAA), Firquat Al Nasr (FAN), and Firquat Tariq bin Zeead (FTZ). Additional Firquats were formed and utilized by SAF later in the conflict. Firquat units were far from ideal indigenous security forces, though highly skilled guerrilla fighters, discipline issues and tribal conflicts plagued their existence. Firqas often refused to conduct operations, especially if it interfered with their agrarian lifestyle.

[132] The term *adoo* translates as enemy in Arabic. Instead of addressing the organization PFLOAG, the term *adoo* was more often used and directly referred to Dhofari tribesmen fighting on the communist side.

[133] Jeapes, *SAS Secret War*, 14, 32, 36-56, 57-70, 102.

(RAF) security personnel, Royal Artillery, and Royal Engineers. Additionally a number of Royal Marines were "seconded" to SAF, further increasing capabilities as well.[134]

In addition to the expansion of SAF and introduction of the SAS, the new Sultan also reached out to neighboring nations for assistance. In response, the Kingdom of Iran contributed the Imperial Iranian Battle Group (IIBG).[135] The Iranian contribution by itself almost doubled the manpower size of the counterinsurgent force in Oman. Additionally, the Iranian contingent further expanded the heliborne capability for resupply and medical evacuation. Though considered to have limited offensive capability, the Iranians provided the preponderance of the static defenses. Likewise, the Hashemite Kingdom of Jordon contributed combat engineers and Special Forces, providing critical support and combat capability. India and others provided smaller support packages to assist also, such as medical teams.[136]

Apart from the increase in forces, conventional counterinsurgency tactics and techniques were applied with great success, most significantly the use of border control measures. Over a few years, successive obstacle belts were constructed, consisting of

---

[134]Gardiner, 25.

[135]Iran, under the Shah Reza Muhammad Pahlavi, was a western ally with especially close ties to the United States. In fact, in 1972 the United States provided Iran with more foreign aid than it did South Vietnam. At the time, Iran and the United States were large trade partners with Iranian oil and petroleum products being exported to the US and American military technologies being exported to Iran. Only after the overthrow of the Shah by Ayatollah Rullah Khomeini in 1979 did US-Iranian national tensions come to light on the world stage.

[136]Akehurst, 36-38.

wire fences and supporting mine fields.[137] The symmetry of Dhofar was well suited for border control due to the geographic contours the region, an ocean to the south and a barren desert to the north. The consecutive "lines" were placed perpendicular to the enemy's LOCs and when coupled with overwatches and heavy patrolling by SAF and IIBG, proved to be a particularly effective means of choking out the enemy's logistics.[138] In addition to the lines, forward outposts established on the border with PDRY with great effect and some population resource controls were implemented.

Augmenting the military initiatives, governmental reforms were executed. Sultan Qaboos, using growing oil revenues, committed substantial funds to developing the country's infrastructure, including transportation, communications, health care, education, and simple needs like water; attacking many of the initial root causes of the insurgency. The socio-political desires suppressed under Sultan Said found fulfillment under Sultan Qaboos. Similarly, the Sultan promoted reconciliation with the adoo and offered a general amnesty for those who would renounce communism and "return" to their families and tribes. The new Sultan though putting great emphasis on military effort, sought to also destroy the favor and support the adoo enjoyed from their own people, making his own governance superior to his opponents.[139]

---

[137]The obstacle belts were known as the Leopard, Hornbeam, Hammer, and Damavand Lines. The Leopard Line was completed in 1971 and manned only a short time. The Hornbeam, Hammer, and Damavand Lines were constructed from 1973 to 1975.

[138]Gardiner, 171.

[139]Akehurst, 15, 19.

Lastly, the counterinsurgency framework held together with a unified aim that permeated all operations. The simple statement of To Secure Dhofar for Civil Development provided a comprehensive understanding for the overall goal of the operation.[140] The motto communicated the insurgency would be defeated through a combination of military force and pacification. To achieve this goal, an SAS veteran who would later also serve SAF, developed the Five Fronts plan. The five fronts plan sought to combat the insurgency holistically through a combination of intelligence, civic development, veterinarian, indigenous security force, and psychological operations.[141] Though originally created for solely for the SAS, the Five Fronts became accepted and formalized through the entire military and civil effort.

PPM Inside the Framework

Nested in the Five Fronts, PPM was not only one of the five pillars of the operational plan but also the pillar that permeated the other four. PPM was vital in communicating the Omani governmental agenda, promoting the milestones of civil development in the pursuit of hearts and minds, shaping the environment to facilitate intelligence collection, and similarly turning the adoo to serve as indigenous local security forces. From the strategic corporal to the Sultan, PPM was understood as vital to combat the insurrection along the jebel.[142]

---

[140]Ibid., 65.

[141]Cole, 36-37.

[142]CF20110914W0001, A former member of the Dhofari Information Service, Interview by Darrell Vaughan and Marcus Welch, London, England, 14 September 2011.

An important note must be made about the hearts and minds campaign in Oman. In modern times, hearts and minds campaigns are often thought of as a function of PPM; persuading the populace of value of the government over the cause of the insurgent. In the context of the period though, PPM was thought of as a facet of the campaign, not the campaign itself.[143] Governmental reforms, services, and development, physical milestones that could be touched and seen, were the basis of hearts and minds. These tangibles, exploited by PPM, and coupled with a persuasive national narrative provided the cumulative hearts and minds campaign.

Similarly, the primary goal of the hearts and minds campaign was more than the winning of popular support but also as shaping the area for intelligence exploitation.[144] At the time of the Dhofar rebellion, as in modern counterinsurgency operations, human intelligence was the key to locating and destroying the enemy. Whether by political buy-in or pragmatic opportunism, hearts and minds provided the canvas that the government's victory narrative was painted on. By persuading the population of the eventual victory of the Sultanate, the tendency of populations to support "the winning side" was exploited and human intelligence opportunities increased as a result.[145]

The PPM campaign itself was executed by a variety of conduits over the course of the war and carried on another five years after the official conclusion of the conflict. Much like the Five Fronts plan, the PPM campaign was primarily the brainchild of one

---

[143]Ibid.

[144]Ibid.

[145]Ibid.

man: John Lane.[146] Lane, as he is referred to as in Major General Tony Jeapes' book *SAS Secret War*, arrived in Oman in 1970 with the first of the SAS troops and remained in country through 1980, although he worked the latter half of his campaign as a civilian in the Sultan's Information Services.[147] As the effort progressed, other British information teams were deployed to Oman in support of the SAS and SAF; however, Lane was the principal Psy Ops orchestrator and continuity for almost a decade.

Naturally, the PPM campaign was not a one man project. Although originating with Lane alone, over time, British Army Information Teams (AITs) rotated in and out of Oman on six month tours. AITs were comprised of a captain and eight to ten men, most of which were initially trained by Lane. The AITs supported the BATTs, who were on similar rotational schedules, and SAF. Afterwards, while working for the Sultan's Information Services, Lane trained and led civilian indigenous teams as well. Civilian teams were primarily specialists though such as radio programmers, newspaper writers, etc. He also counseled and advised the Omani Minister of Information later as well.[148]

Lane and his information teams focused their efforts along three objectives: to support military operational aims; to assist in the military and political defeat of the dissidents; and to persuade the population of the integrity of the Sultan's government. Military operational aims primarily attempted to solicit or induce the adoo, both leaders and foot soldiers, to surrender or "return." PPM was also used in direct support of

---

[146]"John Lane" is a pseudonym. Lane's identity is restricted due to operational security concerns relative to his association with the Special Air Service.

[147]Jeapes, 36.

[148]CF20110914W0001, A former member of the Dhofari Information Service, Interview by Darrell Vaughan and Marcus Welch.

military operations in methods that in modern terms would be called Military Deception (MILDEC), such as creating ruses with false airborne operations and leaflet drops indicating the details of future military raids.[149] Defeating the dissidents militarily and politically was accomplished by communicating factual information of PFLOAG atrocities and defeats (see figure 10). Promoting the integrity of the Sultan's government consisted of advertising development projects and the Sultan's adherence to Islam. Both of these facets possessed substantial appeal to the Dhofari audiences.[150]

Inside these objectives, Lane developed a resounding slogan to permeate all Psy Ops products and programs; "Islam is way, freedom is our aim" became the motto of the conflict to the Dhofaris.[151] The slogan repetitively used on Psy Ops products was the result of detailed counter-propaganda analysis of PRDY's and PFLOAG's propaganda and activities. Communist doctrine of the time included an emphasis on atheism. The doctrine did not resonate with Dhofaris, or the Omani Arabs, whose society and history were deeply engrained with Islam. To reject or deny Allah existed was scandalous in Dhofari culture and those who did usually did so at the barrel of a rifle. The Kalashnikov

---

[149]A major operation was conducted in October of 1971, Operation JAGUAR, with the goal of seizing a point of key terrain on the Jebel. In order to minimalize the number of *adoo* facing the maneuver forces, deceptive measures were employed misguide the *adoo* as to the direction of the attack and to lure the *adoo* away to other defensive positions. A number actions were taken to support the ruse, two of which were executed by the Psy Ops team. First, a leaflet drop was conducted indicating an attack was imminent but providing the wrong direction of attack. Second, 'dummy' parachutists were air-dropped indicating another direction of attack. The leaflet drop and other actions are referenced in Jeapes' *SAS Secret War*, 136. The 'dummy' parachutists is referenced in a personal interview with an anonymous SAS member, dated 19 September 2011.

[150]CF20110914W0001, A former member of the Dhofari Information Service, Interview by Darrell Vaughan and Marcus Welch.

[151]Jeapes, 60.

and other coercive techniques were core to inculcating the Dhofaris to communism. Killings, beatings, maiming, were all PFLOAG tools for spreading control over the Dhofari population. PFLOAG even systematically marched hundreds of Dhofari children to PRDY where starvation, exhaustion, and beatings broke down their wills and re-educated their minds. So the slogan sought to give the Dhofaris back what the communists had taken, Allah and the freedom the semi-nomads were accustomed to.[152] The impact of the slogan came to be known years later when a young Dhofari recited it to Lane, conveying the motto was a traditional saying. Lane acknowledged that it was indeed a traditional saying but one that he had created.[153]

---

[152]Ray, 61-62.

[153]CF20110914W0001, A former member of the Dhofari Information Service, Interview by Darrell Vaughan and Marcus Welch.

To carry the slogan and associated arguments to the Dhofaris, the PPM teams used a number of conventional means; some with creative twists though. The conventional means revolved around radio and leaflet operations as well as mobile cinema. The modified means were the use of notice boards, face to face engagement using proxy speakers, and using word of mouth to reinforce and verify the truthfulness of PPM products.[154]

Radio operations were well suited for the period and region. Dhofar and much of Oman had no communications infrastructure, no electrical production, and little means

_____

[154]Ibid.

for the procurement of non-essential physical possessions. In an effort to access the population, SAF, SAS, and AITs introduced inexpensive Japanese radios to the area. At first the radios were given out freely to the population and later were sold at great discount, assuming the Dhofaris would place greater value on the radios if it cost them something.[155] This led to the creation of broadcasting stations, *Radio Dhofar* and *Radio Oman*, which brought the Sultan's governmental message to the mountain people. Lane and information team, primarily staffed by indigenous personnel, used broadcasting and the transistor radios to highlight the civil development being conducted, differentiate the government of Qaboos from the government of Said, present turned adoo appeals to encourage current adoo to return, and encourage adherence to Islam through the preaching of Imams-all countering the communist narrative.[156] Sultan Qaboos even personally broadcast on occasion, adding great authority to the broadcasting.[157] Most significantly, the radio stations facilitated a method to directly counter propaganda coming from PDRY. PFLOAG's primary means of disseminating propaganda was through *Radio Aden* which broadcast into Dhofar. Though exaggerated and focused on party-line politics, Radio Aden was listened to. Mimicking PFLOAG's method, yet adding verifiable truthfulness, effectively countered PFLOAG's messaging.[158]

---

[155]Jeapes, 37.

[156]CF20110914W0001, A former member of the Dhofari Information Service, Interview by Darrell Vaughan and Marcus Welch.

[157]Ray, 87, 202-205.

[158]Akehurst, 30, 80.

The PPM teams also ran extensive leaflet operations, encouraging defection, unveiling the "guised motives" of the PFLOAG agenda, contrasting Islam with communism, conveying governmental improvements, and arguing the inevitable victory of the Sultan (see figure 12). Though no statistical records exist to quantify the effectiveness of the drops, specific incidents of adoo surrendering with a leaflet in hand are many. Key to the effectiveness of the defection appeal was the understanding of the cultural dishonor associated with surrender. To counter this value, appeals were never made for surrender but rather for reconciliation. The adoo were beckoned to return their tribal structure, to their families, and to Allah. To assist in maintaining honor, the adoo were also requested to join a firqat and fight for the Sultan. Payment for their service was also offered, including bounties for weapons and information. Sidestepping the surrender term, proved very effective.[159] Some leaflets did not include an appeal to surrender but rather instructions on how to surrender. Simple pictographic instructions illustrated to the adoo where to go for reconciliation and how to present themselves safely. Key to the effectiveness of these operations was the follow-on treatment of SEPs. SEPs, when appropriately returned to their tribes, sent messages back to their adoo peers reinforcing the truthfulness of the leaflets.

Notice boards were also used in common points of transition. Similar to the billboards of today, notice boards were placed in high traffic areas, in particular entrances to markets, known as Souks, and at traffic control checkpoints. Primarily, civil development projects were emphasized on notice boards, reinforcing what Sultanate's

---

[159]Jeapes, 39.

civil development programs or explaining population resource control measures. Though the population was predominately illiterate, passers-by could ask soldiers on guard or local "letter writers" about the message.[160]

Face to face persuasion was also a crucial means, especially effective when making use of proxies. Although it might appear odd to the westerner, the firquats often spoke with the adoo directly as they were often family, extended family, or tribe. The adoo were at times persuaded by quasi-peer voices to "come over" to the government's side. Once again although statistical data does not exist, multiple anecdotes do. The best known example took place at a small coastal city called Sudh, in 1971. There, in order to test out the nascent firquat application, a firquat accompanied by a few SAS men entered Sudh in force. Instead of attacking the adoo directly though, the firquat summoned the towns' people and articulated the value of supporting the Sultan over the communists. Afterwards, the firquat beckoned the adoo and spoke directly with their enemy as well. In the course of several hours of conversation, the firquat-not the SAS men, were able to persuade the adoo to "come-over." As a result, the firquat number in Sudh doubled in one day, without a shot being fired. The use of indigenous personnel to persuade proved invaluable as they leveraged existing credibility that external forces rarely possess.[161]

Similarly, word of mouth was used to convey talking points or reinforce the truthfulness of other products. In modern terms, this type of dissemination is referred to

---

[160]Literacy was rare in Dhofar; however, larger villages had designated 'letter writers' who wrote or read letters for the village as required. After a period of trial and error, local 'letter writers' were officially hired by the AITs or Information Services to read notice boards to the villages on prescribed schedules. See Jeapes, 38.

[161]Jeapes, 71-81.

as whisper campaigns or rumor campaigns. The technique proved especially useful in

Dhofar as customary greetings often adhered to a prescribed format:

> "Peace be upon you"
> "And on you peace"
> "How is your health"
> "Fine, praise be to Allah. And your?"
> "Fine also, praise be to Allah. What is the news?"[162]

Because literacy was minimal and electronic communications unheard of prior to the

introduction of the transistor radios, this cultural news gathering was custom in any

Dhofari society. Although this dissemination technique was used for delivering specific

messaging at times, it was primarily heuristically used reinforce formal products and

lines of persuasion.[163] Using informal communications, adoo could verify the truthfulness

of leaflets and radio broadcasts.[164]

Mobile cinemas were also used systematically in conjunction with Civic Action

Teams (CATs) to promote the Sultan's development programs and denounce

communism.[165] The films were not propaganda productions but rather commercial films

used as lures to draw the indigenous population to a central location. Before or after the

showing of a film such as *Zulu*, government officials or Firquats addressed those gathered

---

[162]Ray, 56.

[163]Supporting Operation JAGUAR in 1971, SAS deliberately spread news of the operation via *word of mouth* as referenced in Jeapes' *SAS: Secret War*, 136.

[164]CF20110914W0001, A former member of the Dhofari Information Service, Interview by Darrell Vaughan and Marcus Welch.

[165]Civic Action Teams were SAS teams augmented with civil specialists such as veterinarians, doctors, and engineers. CATs were similar to current Civil Affairs Teams.

and delivered talking points. In Dhofar, where electricity existed in only three or four towns, the viewing of a film was a major event.[166]

The PPM teams also exploited specific adoo atrocities by numerous means simply by reinforcing the truth. The SAS and SAF decided at an early stage to conduct only truthful PPM and eventually established a reputation for truthfulness. The attribute contrasted greatly with the communist propaganda being broadcast from PDRY. Since many of the adoo listening to the radio also participated in the operations promoted, the untruthfulness of the station became apparent. Exploiting this facet, when communist or adoo atrocities were broadcast, the broadcast was accepted as true.[167] Although many adoo atrocities were exploited by the PPM teams and the Information Services, two incidents were exceptionally noteworthy. The first occurred when a disgruntled adoo was given a letter and ordered to deliver it to a PFLOAG base located across the border in PDRY. Instead of delivering the letter, the adoo surrendered to a Firquat along the way. The letter the illiterate adoo was to deliver turned out to be his own death warrant; he was to be executed for substandard performance. Seizing the opportunity, the adoo was solicited to tell his story nationwide by broadcasting it on radio. The second incident similarly exhibited the values of PFLOAG. After firefight with SAF, two adoo were gravely wounded and could not travel. The adoo leader decided to execute them in order to guard them from capture. After some pleading though, the wounded adoo were left to die but only after being stripped of all clothing and weapons. SAF found the wounded

---

[166]CF20110914W0001, A former member of the Dhofari Information Service, Interview by Darrell Vaughan and Marcus Welch.

[167]Ibid.

adoo though before their demise, treated their wounds, and both lived. Again seizing the opportunity, both adoo agreed to broadcast their experiences in order to encourage defection. In this case, photographs were taken, leaflets made, and a leaflet drop was conducted for their comrades to see their fate.

PPM Summary: The Dhofar Rebellion

The Dhofar Campaign did eventually come to an end. In 1975, the rebellion was officially declared over, although occasional fighting flared up for another few years. The five fronts of the campaign did cripple the adoo's capabilities, the sealane choke points were protected, and the Sultanate became an even stronger and more stable ally. The counterinsurgency operation was a success and partially due to the PPM support.

When looking at the classic counterinsurgent synthesis chart from Chapter 3 of this thesis, John Lane's aims and efforts closely resemble the picture. His aim of "persuade the population of the integrity of the Sultan's government," is exactly in line with the classic counterinsurgent's primary aim of "sway the population to the support the government over the insurgent." Likewise, the Dhofar PPM campaign addressed every one of the applicable principles (agit-prop may not have applied to this scenario). A comprehensive reconciliation program was run to "turn" the adoo to support the government. The program was credibly reinforced by statements and appeals of adoo who had "returned" to their families, the government, and Allah. Propaganda of Deed was conducted providing tangible schools, wells, roads, markets, and payments for firquat service. PPM was employed to support HUMINT in general terms of shaping a positive image of the Sultan's government and in specific measures such as the letter boxes. PDRY support was unveiled to reveal the masked Marxist-Atheist agenda which

86

was not compatible with the Dhofari way of life. In detail, specific incidences were exploited to supplement to unveiling, such as adoo carrying his own death warrant. Also, in this particular instance, the Sultan's Ministry of Information, was successful in running the PPM although with John Lane's assistance and with military AIT and aviation support.

Many factors undoubtedly contributed to the success of the COIN operation in Dhofar; from geography to government, a host of dynamics came into play. In the context of the framework, PPM was employed elaborately and effectively for achieving the prescribed aims. From Major General Jeapes to Corporal Lane, notable counterinsurgents viewed PPM not just as an important element of the operation but as a pivotal if not paramount tool in the effort. In the following chapter, PPM is applied on an exponentially grander scale but with more contentious results.

CHAPTER 5

COIN PPM OF THE VIETNAM WAR

Yet despite a major and persistent effort, including bringing psychological warfare experts from the United States, results were disappointing. Except for an occasional platoon-size group, most defectors were individuals. Mass surrenders never developed despite our intense psychological warfare efforts, which apparently could not overcome the enemy's intensive indoctrination.

—General William C. Westmoreland,
A Soldier Reports

But I could see that actual conditions in the Vietnamese countryside were beyond his experience and therefore his understanding.

—Rufus Phillips, *Why Vietnam Matters*

The key to the Vietcong success in South Vietnam during the present war has been their political subversive underground organization, built up over many years and firmly rooted within the country during the earlier French Indo-China War. In a People's Revolutionary War, and Vietnam is no exception, the primary weapon is the underground organization within the population. The secondary weapon is the guerrilla forces which depend upon the underground organization for all their requirements, but which, at the same time, support the advance of the underground organization into the heart of the threatened government and country. The political aim is, therefore, dominant and guerrilla operations are designed to achieve political rather than military results.

—Sir Robert Thompson, *No Exit From Vietnam*

Context of the Conflict

In contrast to the Dhofar Rebellion studied in the previous chapter, the Vietnam

War was infinitely more complex in terms of scale, scope, and intensity. Also

contrasting, the COIN operation of the Dhofar Rebellion is considered as successful

while the COIN operation in the Vietnam War is commonly viewed as a failure. Many of

the tactics that were applied in each were similar, including the PPM operations, yet many results differed. To understand how the conditions affected the tactics and influenced the outcome, the context of the war must be examined.[168]

The first step in understanding the Vietnam War is acknowledging a more appropriate title: the Second Indochina War.[169] Although conventional American combat troops entered the war in 1965, for the Vietnamese, the war started in 1946 in the aftermath of the Second World War. Up to that point, Vietnam, Laos, and Cambodia had been collectively known as French Indochina since 1893 when France conquered and occupied the areas and declared the regions as protectorates. As a result of the Second World War though, Indochinese governing authority was usurped by the Japanese and later recovered by the French again, albeit in a weakened state. Political and economic turmoil wracked post-war France providing an opportunity for revolutionary action in

---

[168]The area of operations was far greater in the Vietnam War than in the Dhofar Rebellion, as were the sizes of forces employed and combated. The corridor through which enemy lines of communication (LOCs) passed between the People's Democratic Republic of Yemen (PRDY) and the Sultanate of Oman amounted to roughly fifty miles; whereas the LOC corridor between Cambodia and Laos and the Republic of Vietnam, known as the Ho Chi Minh trail, exceeded six hundred miles. Similarly, while the opposing force in Dhofar consisted of approximately five thousand insurgents and supporters at its height, hundreds of thousands insurgents and their supporters participated in the Vietnam War. Correspondingly, the United Kingdom's military presence in Oman was minimal, measured in hundreds. The United States' military presence in Vietnam though numbered over half a million at its peak.

[169]Failing to understand historical precursors is common in American political and military endeavors. For the example, the 'Persian Gulf War' of 1991 is referred to in the Arab world as the 'Second Persian Gulf War' as a reference to the Iran-Iraq War of 1980-1988 which triggered the 1991 war. Likewise, the current war in Afghanistan is commonly understood to have started in 2001, whereas the depth of the conflict extends back to the 1979 Soviet invasion followed by the Afghan civil war from 1992 to 1996 or possibly as late as 2001.

Vietnam. An independence movement immediately took hold and the First Indochina War initiated.[170]

Through the political and military efforts of a group of communist inspired Vietnamese nationalists, collectively known as the Viet Minh, over the course of eight years, the French were driven from Vietnam.[171] The Viet Minh's key architects, Ho Chi Minh and Vo Nguyen Giap, were students of Mao Tse Tung's revolutionary warfare methods and successfully applied a version of his protracted war theory.[172] This conflict resulted in the Geneva Agreements of 1954, which divided the Vietnam into two provisional entities at the seventeenth parallel.[173] The northern government, the Democratic Republic of Vietnam (DRV), received the support of the USSR and the Peoples Republic of China (PRC); while the southern government, the Republic of Vietnam (RVN), was backed by the US. The agreement stipulated elections would be held in 1956 to reunite the country under one government. Those elections were never

---

[170]John Pimlott, "Ho Chi Minh's Triumph," *War in Peace: Conventional and Guerrilla Warfare Since 1945*; Thompson, *War In Peace*, 61-62.

[171]*Viet Minh* translates to "the Vietnamese People."

[172]Mao Tse Tung's 'protracted war' warfare strategy consists of three phases: (1) Organization, Consolidation, and Preservation; (2) Progressive Expansion, and (3) Decisive or Destruction of the Enemy. In protracted war, a guerrilla force uses time, space, and will as weapons to gradually wear down an opponent. Ho Chi Minh and Vo Nguyen Giap mimicked and modified the 'protracted war' theory to war in Vietnam against the French, against the Republic of Vietnam (South Vietnam), and against the US. See Mao Tse-Tung, *On Guerrilla Warfare*, trans. Samuel B. Griffith II (Champaign, IL: University of Illinois Press, 1961), 21-22, 46, 95, 98; Mao Tse-Tung, *Selected Writings of Mao Tse Tung* (Peking: Foreign Languages Press, 1972), 208-219.

[173]The Geneva Agreements not only divided north and South Vietnam, it also declared Cambodia and Laos independent of French rule.

held though[174] and a renewal of guerrilla activity ensued in 1959, initiating the Second Indochina War.[175]

Between 1956 and 1965, the political and military viability of South Vietnam was less than stable. Internal political struggles, religious confrontations, ineffective governmental reforms, and dependency on foreign aid plagued the nascent government.[176] Exacerbating the situation, using the remnants of the Viet Minh remaining in the south, North Vietnam commenced unconventional warfare operations against the south agitating with the newly branded Viet Cong.[177] Through the tumultuous period, the US attempted to provide a guiding and supporting hand to South Vietnamese, with a host of governmental and military advisors as well as related aid packages.[178] Yet

---

[174]Knowing an open election would result in a victory for the communists due to the greater population of North Vietnam, South Vietnam's President Ngo Dinh Diem refused to permit the reunification elections of 1956 to occur. This decision was supported by the US President, Dwight Eisenhower. See Robert Thompson. "Vietnam: The clash between the Republic of South Vietnam and communist insurgents rapidly involved the worlds' greatest power in a war it could not win." Thompson and Keegan, *War in Peace*, 181.

[175]Pimlott, 61-80.

[176]For a more thorough understanding of the turmoil of the Republic of Vietnam prior to 1965, See Rufus Phillips, *Why Vietnam Matters*; and William E. Colby, *Lost Victory, A Firsthand Account of America's Sixteen-Year Involvement in Vietnam* (Chicago: Contemporary Books, 1989).

[177]Viet Cong translates to "Vietnamese Communists." Apart from Viet Cong, the terms the National Liberation Front (NLF) and the Provisional Revolutionary Government of South Vietnam (PRG) were also used. 'NLF' was adopted in 1960 and replaced with 'PRG' in 1969, Viet Cong though was the term most commonly used to describe the southern Vietnamese communist organization. James S. Olson, *Dictionary of the Vietnam War* (New York: Greenwood Press, 1988), 470-471.

[178]The US established the Military Advisory Assistance Group (MAAG) in South Vietnam in 1956 to assist in building South Vietnam's military capacity. It was augmented by the Temporary Equipment Recovery Mission (TERM) for supplying the

all the efforts to stabilize the country and deter communist aggression fell short. After a presidential assassination,[179] a series of coups, a number of Viet Cong attacks on US installations,[180] and the Gulf of Tonkin incident,[181] the US initiated air strikes against North Vietnam in 1964 and committed combat ground troops to South Vietnam in 1965.[182] For the next seven years, the conflict became an American war.

Eleven years before the "American war," the US Saigon Military Mission (SMM) and the Military Advisory Assistance Group (MAAG) were established to assist the fledgling Government of RVN (GVN). SMM was a small US Central Intelligence Agency (CIA) element and MAAG a larger wholly military group. With the SMM and MAAG, came assistance in psychological operations. In fact, US PPM support, started in

---

military. By the end of 1956, South Vietnam was receiving two hundred and seventy millions dollars in annual aid, making it the third largest per capita recipient of US aid. William S. Turley, *The Second Indochina War: A Concise Political and Military History* (New York: Rowman and Littlefield Publishers Inc., 2009), 30-33.

[179]Ngo Dinh Diem, the President of South Vietnam from since 1954, was assassinated in November 1963 in a coup led by General Duong Van Minh. The coup received the tacit support of the US and was followed by more political instability in successive coups. Ironically, US President John F. Kennedy, who had sanctioned the coup and indirectly Diem's assassination, was also assassinated in the same month.

[180]The Viet Cong attacked the US advisory compound at Kontum City, bombed the American frequented Kinh Do Theater, sank the U.S.S. Card while berthed in Siagon, attacked the Nam Dong US Special Forces compound, mortared the US Bien Hoa airbase, attacked US billeting at Qui Nhon, and attacked the Pleiku US airbase in a series of provoking gestures in 1964 and early 1965. Phillip B. Davidson, *Vietnam at War: The History 1946-1975* (Novato, CA: Presidio Press, 1988), 313, 316, 323, 333, 336.

[181]On 2, 4, and 5 August, 1964, the 'Gulf of Tonkin' incident occurred where engagements took place between North Vietnamese torpedo boats and the *U.S.S. Maddox* and the *U.S.S. Turner Joy*. Davidson, 317-320.

[182]The first US airstrike on North Vietnam occurred on the 5 August, 1964. The first US 'combat' ground troops arrived in South Vietnam on the 10 March 1965. At the time, the Marines were requested as airfield security forces. Davidson, 320, 343-344.

Indochina as early as 1954.[183] The G-5 PSYWAR staff division of the Franco-Vietnamese Army, the interim government, and the newly established GVN all received assistance in conducting PPM. Among other operations, SMM and US Information Agency (USIA)/US Information Service (USIS) applied psychological techniques against the *Viet Minh* to disrupt their takeover of Hanoi in 1955, in extensive pacification efforts of the south, and even to influence the 1955 RVN elections.[184] Most notably, psychological operations were essential in compelling over nine hundred thousand North Vietnamese Catholics to resettle to the south in 1954, protecting the Catholics from communist oppression while increasing the support base of Catholic President Diem.[185]

An important note must be established here about the "American War" as counterinsurgency effort. The war was a counterinsurgency operation with the objective of preserving the legitimacy of the Republic of Vietnam (RVN) with preponderance of combat being fought against South Vietnamese insurgents, the Viet Cong. Yet the war was a "dual war" in which North Vietnamese Army (NVA) units fought as well.[186] As early as 1964, NVA units infiltrated into South Vietnam,[187] and a number of conventional

---

[183]Robert W. Chandler, *War of Ideas: The U.S. Propaganda Campaign in Vietnam* (Boulder, CO: Westview Press, Inc., 1981), 14.

[184]Lansdale, 137-139, 161-162, 224-227, 333.

[185]William C. Westmoreland, *A Soldier Reports* (New York: Da Capo Press, Inc. 1976), 52; Robert J. Kodosky, *Psychological Operations American Style: The Joint United States Public Affairs Office, Vietnam and Beyond* (New York: Lexington Books, 2007), 91-94.

[186]The North Vietnamese Army (NVA) was also known as the People's Army of Vietnam (PAVN).

[187]By December of 1964, at least three North Vietnamese Infantry Regiments were infiltrating into the Central Highlands of South Vietnam. By the spring of 1965, the

battles were fought against them, such as the battles of Ia Drang and Khe Sanh.[188] In fact

at the end of the war in 1975, it was the NVA who delivered the coup de grace not the

Viet Cong. By 1975 though, the "American War" was had been over for two years.

Likewise, substantial US air and naval campaigns were directed against the DRV in an

attempt to degrade support provided to the Viet Cong. Nonetheless, while major

conventional combat operations were directed against the military and infrastructure of

the DRV, counterinsurgency against the Viet Cong was the principal operation during

direct US involvement from 1965 to 1972. General William C. Westmoreland,

commander of Military Assistance Command Vietnam (MACV) from 1964 to 1968,

recounts the primacy of counterinsurgency in his memoirs:

> Pacification was the ultimate goal of the Americans and the South Vietnamese
> government. A complex task involving military, psychological, political, and
> economic factors, its aim was to achieve an economically and politically viable
> society in which the people could live without constant fear of death or physical
> harm. It was an effort to improve the quality of life, to improve sanitation,
> drainage, roads, pagodas, schools, teachers, dispensaries, communications
> facilities, administrative offices; and to enable the people to pursue their
> occupations: fishing, tilling the land, raising water buffalo, chickens, pigs, and
> bring produce to market. Fundamental to pacification was security, and as long as
> insurgents were raiding, robbing, molesting, and killing in South Vietnam, the
> government forces would have to spend their time keeping the enemy out of the
> hamlets and villages rather than improving the welfare of the people.[189]

---

entire 325th Division of the North Vietnamese Army (NVA) had infiltrated. Davidson,
324-329.

[188]Mai Elliot, *RAND in Southeast Asia: A History of the Vietnam War Era* (Santa
Monica, CA: RAND Corporation, 2010), 145; John Prados, *The History of an
Unwinnable War, 1945-1975* (Lawrence, KS: University Press of Kansas, 2009), 227-
230, 240-241.

[189]Westmoreland, *A Soldier Reports*, 68-69.

Framework of the Counterinsurgency, 1965 to 1972

MAAG was replaced by the expanded Military Assistance Command Vietnam (MACV) in 1962. MACV was a joint military headquarters command, including US Air Force, Navy, and Marine Corps; responsible for directing and coordinating all US military activity in South Vietnam. MACV was only one arm of the entire United States Mission though; MACV was subordinate to the US ambassador and working in conjunction with several non-military agencies such as the United States Information Agency (USIA)/United States Information Service (USIS), the Central Intelligence Agency (CIA), the Agency for International Development (AID), and others. The organizations collectively, and in cooperation with South Vietnamese peer organizations, constituted the comprehensive framework of the counterinsurgency effort. According to General Westmoreland, "it was a complex, awkward arrangement."[190]

Awkward as it may have been, MACV was the primary action arm of the counterinsurgency effort. Growing from a few thousand troops in 1962, by the end of 1968 MACV amassed troop strength of over half a million. The MACV footprint eventually covered all of South Vietnam and was divided among four Vietnamese Corps Tactical Zones (CTZs) for command and control purposes.[191] While responsible for

---

[190]Ibid., 74-75.

[191]From north to south, RVN was administratively organized into Corps Tactical Zones (CTZ) for both military operations and RVN governance. I Corps was the northernmost zone. II Corps second most northern, focused on the central highlands; it was the largest zone yet least populated. III Corps included the areas surrounding Saigon but not Saigon itself which was a separate independent command. IV Corps was the southernmost zone and focused on the Mekong Delta. See Westmoreland. *A Soldier Reports*, 58. For graphical understanding of the CTZs and how US and Vietnamese units were arrayed by year see Shelby L. Stanton, *Vietnam Order of Battle* (Washington, DC: U.S. News Books, 1983), Appendix F.

combating the NVA and Viet Cong militarily, MACV was also made responsible for all

US pacification efforts with the establishment of the Civil Operations and Revolutionary

Development Support (CORDS) organization early in 1967.[192] In addition to size, reach,

and responsibility, MACV also had continuity in command. From 1964 to 1972, MACV

had only two commanders: General William Westmoreland and General Creighton

Abrams.[193] Although national strategies evolved with time and circumstance, Generals

Westmoreland and Abrams remained the primary orchestrators of applied strategy.

Over the course of the war, three major evolutions in strategy occurred. In the

early years, under General Westmoreland, the efforts were categorized as "big unit war"

with pacification secondary. Westmoreland's strategy sought to (1) protect logistical

bases, (2) initiate, penetrate, and eliminate enemy base camps and sanctuaries, and (3)

conduct sustained ground combat operations to destroy NVA and Viet Cong main force

units while simultaneously increasing the capability of the Army of the Republic of

---

[192]The term pacification refers to the aspect of counterinsurgency designed to win
the allegiance of a population from an insurgent force through means of governmental
authoritative actions such as agricultural assistance, health initiatives, educational
reforms, public works, security provisions, and similar projects. 'Pacification' is also
referred to as 'Revolutionary Development.' In RVN, pacification efforts started in 1963
with the Vietnamese led program called HOP TAC or 'cooperation' in Vietnamese. HOP
TAC was expanded in 1966 and evolved into the Vietnamese Ministry of Revolutionary
Development. Likewise, both the US Department of State (DoS) and MACV developed
similar organizations. DoS created the Office of Civil Operations (OCO) and MACV
established a Revolutionary Development Support Directorate. In early 1967, MACV
assumed responsibility for all US pacification efforts, amalgamating all US efforts into
one organization: Civil Operations and Revolutionary Development Support (CORDS).
Ironically, though controlled by MACV, a civilian appointee headed CORDS.
Westmoreland, *A Soldier Reports*, 210-216; Elliot, 282.

[193]General Westmoreland commanded MACV from June 1964 to July 1968.
General Abrams commanded MACV from July 1968 to June 1972. Olson, *Dictionary*, 2-
3, 485-486.

Vietnam (ARVN) and conducting pacification operations. According to Westmoreland, based on the political constraints, the strategy was "essentially that of a war of attrition."[194] This was the strategy from late 1965 until 1968.

Circumstances and strategies shifted in 1968. Two major events occurred in 1968: the first Tet Offensive[195] and the command of MACV changed. The Tet Offensive changed the course of the war. Militarily, the combined Viet Cong and NVA offensive was a disaster for the Vietnamese communists. The Viet Cong suffered a major loss of manpower and failed to provoke a general uprising. The magnitude of the offensive shocked the US public and fed a massive shift in political support against the US war effort. Also following the offensive, General Abrams took command of MACV and modified Westmoreland's strategy. Abram's strategy was known as the clear and hold and one-war strategy where the US and RVN armies continued large scale combat operations but placed additional emphasis on pacification.[196] A key aspect of the one-war strategy was the Accelerated Pacification Campaign (APC), which applied extensive

---

[194]See Westmoreland, *A Soldier Reports*, 145, 149, 153; Turley, 97-100.

[195]The first major Tet Offensive initiated on the 30th of January in 1968; a second major Tet Offensive occurred a year later. Two "mini-Tets" occurred in between them. The first Tet Offensive consisted of simultaneous attacks on most of South Vietnam's major cities and towns, primarily by Viet Cong units. Most notably, battles in the historic cities of Saigon and Hue (pronounced 'Wayh') occurred lasting weeks. In a synchronized diversion, two NVA/PAVN divisions laid siege to the US Marine outpost at Khe Sanh in I CTZ beginning on the 21st of January 1968 in order to divert the attention of US forces. The Vietnamese communists expected to generate a general uprising, none manifested however. Davidson, 473-525; Turley, 137-156.

[196]Elliot, 328-335.

resources toward development and employed Vietnamese paramilitary forces to clear and

hold, though a GVN program.[197]

The tactical aspects of General Abram's one-war strategy continued throughout

the American involvement in the war; however, in 1969 political shifts changed the

comprehensive efforts and strategy for the war with concept of Vietnamization. In June

1969, the new mission of MACV focused on building up the Republic of Vietnam Armed

Forces (RVNAF) in manpower, material, and tactical competence. RVNAF was to take

lead and US combat forces gradually redeploy. Over the next three years, RVNAF

reached its greatest height in material and cadre. The war effort expanded, including

operations in Cambodia and Laos in an attempt to degrade infiltration of NVA forces and

diminish supply efforts to the Viet Cong. During the same period, US combat forces

reduced in size from over five hundred thousand to fewer than fifty thousand before the

US declared a cease fire and finalized peace agreements with the DRV in January

1973.[198] The war continued for the South Vietnamese though and on the 30 April 1975,

the Republic of Vietnam ceased to exist.

---

[197] APC started in November 1968, being initiated after the decimation of *Viet Cong* due to the militarily failed Tet offensive. APC was organizationally supported by recently established Civil Operations and Revolutionary Development Support (CORDS) organization created under MACV in 1967. In APC, the 'clear and hold' forces used were primarily Regional Forces (RF) and Popular Forces (PF), commonly referred to as 'roughs' and 'puffs.' RF/PFs were part of the RVN Territorial Forces who primarily focused on the static defenses of villages, hamlets, and infrastructure. PFs were usually not uniformed but a localized 'home guard'. See Elliot, 329; Olson, 4-5, 374, 388-389.

[198] Davidson, 531-532; Turley, 182-183.

PPM Inside the Framework

Just as the Vietnam War provided the largest expenditure of aerial ordnance of any American conflict to date, the war also saw the largest utilization of PPM. In terms of organization, effort, people, and products, the degree of influence efforts was unprecedented and remains unsurpassed. Civilian information services and military PPM organizations were employed on grand scales using established and developing techniques. The US-USSR Cold War propaganda battles of the 1950s;[199] the PPM novelties of Malaya, Algeria, and Huk-Philippine counterinsurgency operations;[200] the effects of "red" PPM experienced by US prisoners of war in the Korean conflict; and the flurry of early irregular warfare theory developed at the US Army Psychological Warfare

---

[199]In early years of the Cold War the need for PPM was recognized. In 1948 the US Congress passed the US Information and Educational Exchange Act, Public Law 80-402 (commonly known as the Smith-Mundt Act), authorizing for the first time, funding for international radio programming to promote 'a better understanding of the United States in other countries'. Effort intensified at the outbreak of the Korean Conflict in 1950, with President Harry Truman's initiation of the 'Campaign of Truth' to extol the virtues of democracy and denounce Soviet socialism. In 1953 President Dwight Eisenhower created the US Information Agency (USIA) to further expand the effort (note: The USIA existed until 1999 when USIA responsibilities were transferred to the Department of State). Decades of international propaganda battles followed but were most blatant during the 'red scare' of the 1950s. See Robert E. Summers, ed., *America's Weapons of Psychological Warfare* (New York: H.W. Wilson Company, 1951), 11-14; Ron D. McLaurin, "U.S. Organization for Psychological Operations," in *Military Propaganda, Psychological Warfare and Operations,* ed. Ron D. McLaurin (New York: Praeger Publishers, 1982), 66-71.

[200]The British Malaya Emergency (1948-1960), the French Algerian Revolution (1954-1962), and the Philippine Hukbalahap Rebellion (1946-1954) were counterinsurgency operations occurring just prior to US combat involvement in South Vietnam. Each conflict included considerable psychological warfare campaigns and was studied in great detail by several 'counterinsurgency experts' such as Sir Robert Thompson, David Galula, and Edward Lansdale. Each of these 'experts' participated in one of the previous COIN operations but were also actors in Vietnam to differing degrees. See chapter 2 of this thesis and Chandler, 14-15.

Center[201] created opportunity and demand to apply the US's expanded PPM capabilities, especially in a counterinsurgency operation.

PPM Organization

As General Westmoreland indicated about the awkwardness of the organizational structure of MACV, the PPM organizational structure was likewise complex. USIA/USIS was the lead US organization for conducting any informational campaign in RVN prior to deployment of US combat units, yet only one of many organizations engaged in influence activities. This changed during 1965. To synchronize the greatly expanding psychological efforts of USIA/USIS, AID, MACV, RVNAF, and the Vietnamese Information Service (VIS), President Johnson's administration created the Joint United States Public Affairs Office (JUSPAO). JUSPAO was essentially an upgrade of the existing USIS in South Vietnam, but staffed with additional AID and MACV augmentees. The director of USIS-Vietnam became the director of JUSPAO and the organization was given the responsibility of operating and coordinating all US civil and military PPM and informational campaigns in RVN. The JUSPAO was therefore not solely a PPM entity; it also maintained a Public Affairs function and provided a centralized headquarters for all PPM in RVN.[202]

---

[201]The US Army Psychological Warfare Center was founded in 1952 and later became the US Army Special Warfare Center in 1956. It was at the center that nascent US Army doctrine for irregular warfare was developed, including guerrilla warfare and psychological warfare. Paddock, *US Army Special Warfare,* 140-150.

[202]For additional background on the establishment and responsibilities of the JUSPAO see Kodosky. *Psychological Operations American Style*, xiv, 4, 16-18; Robert E. Elder, *The Information Machine: The United States Information Agency and American Foreign Policy* (Syracuse, NY: Syracuse University Press, 1968), 20; John W.

By itself, JUSPAO was a complex organization, consisting of five major departments: Office of the Director, Information, Cultural Affairs, North Vietnamese Affairs, Technical Services, and Field Development, and additionally was peer-partnered with VIS. JUSPAO was sizable; at its peak it possessed a staff of over six hundred American and Vietnamese employees, rivaling its military counterparts. Apart from JUSPAO's executive responsibilities, the organization conducted PSYOP in direct and advisory roles, primarily using mass media outlets such as RVN's *Voice of Freedom* and the overt US *Voice of America* radio stations. JUSPAO delved into television, supporting *Truyen Hinh Viet Nam*, a GVN television station, in 1965. Similarly, JUSPAO created a number of printed products such as the *Ngon Song* newspaper, and the *Huong Que*, *Gioi Tu-Do*, *Long Ne*, and *Van Tac Vu* magazines.[203] Using mass media, JUSPAO focused primarily on strategic and national level PPM. [204]

Synchronization and coordination were also the responsibilities of JUSPAO. From the US ambassador to the Field Forces, numerous levels of planners, integrators, and executers were instrumental in the cumulative PSYOP effort. Still four key organizations were critical to PSYOP under the JUSPAO's directive guidance: the 4th Psychological Operations Group (POG), the 7th POG, the 7th US Air Force, and the Civil Operations and Revolutionary Development Support Psychological Operations

---

Henderson, *The United States Information Agency* (New York: Frederick A. Praeger Publishers, 1969), 243-262.

[203] *Houng Que*, meaning 'rural spirit' and *Gioi Tu-Do*, meaning 'free world,' magazines were printed on a monthly basis. *Long Ne*, meaning 'mother's heart,' and *Van Tac Vu*, meaning 'cultural drama,' were printed bi-monthly.

[204] Chandler, 135-139; Kodosky, 135-139.

Division (CORDS/POD). 4th POG was the primary tactical PPM provider in-country while 7th POG supported PSYOP with print and production capabilities. The 7th US Air Force (USAF) provided air support for leaflet operations, aerial loudspeaker operations, and occasional special services. CORDS/POD was the lead for pacification efforts.[205]

On the ground in RVN, the bulk of PPM activity was conducted by MACV's psychological arm, the 4th POG; albeit, the "in-country" PPM capability required time to build. Provisionally spearheaded by detachments and companies from the 7th POG, it took until early 1966 to establish a functioning psychological operations battalion, the 6th Psychological Operations Battalion (POB) in the RVN. Responding to increasing demands and growing relative to the total force build-up, in December 1967 a full PSYOP group was established and remained in-country through the end of 1971. The 4th POG consisted of four POBs: 6th POB, 7th POB, 8th POB, and 10th POB, allocating one POB to each Field Force/CTZ. The 4th POG was, in effect, the command and control center for all tactical PSYOP in Vietnam for the four middle years, 1967 to 1971.[206]

Established on Okinawa in 1965, elements of 7th POG provided the initial tactical PSYOP support to MACV until 4th POG was established. However, its primary

---

[205]U.S. Department of the Army, Army Concept Team in Vietnam (ACTIV), "Employment of US Psychological Operations Units in Vietnam," 7 July 1969, II-3, II-4.

[206]4th POG was based in Tan Son Nhut, serving in RVN from December 1967 to October 1971. 6th POB was based in Tan Son Nhut followed by Bien Hoa, serving in RVN from February 1966 to June 1971. 7th POB was based in Nha Trang followed by Da Nang, serving in RVN from December 1967 to December 1971. 8th POB was based in Nha Trang followed by Pleiku, serving in RVN from December 1967 to June 1971. 10th POB was based in Can Tho, serving in RVN from December 1967 to April 1971. Additionally, four separate PSYOP companies (19th, 244th, 245th, and 246th) served in RVN starting in 1966, each of which formed the nucleus of a later POB. Stanton, 237-238.

contribution throughout the conflict was print and production support. To facilitate

support, 7th POG maintained a liaison detachment in Saigon co-located with the 4th POG

headquarters.[207] Apart from production support, 7th POG also provided PSYOP specific

intelligence and analysis such as monitoring of communist media outlets.[208]

The Air Force contribution to the PSYOP effort was provided by the 7th USAF,

primarily by the 5th and 9th Special Operations Squadrons (SOS) of the 14th Special

Operations Wing.[209] Many USAF elements supported PPM missions on an ad hoc basis;

however, the 5th and 9th SOS was specially tailored and dedicated support for

psychological operations within RVN. Fitted with loudspeaker systems and specialized

chutes for disseminating leaflets, approximately forty aircraft serviced PPM missions in

the four CTZs routinely.[210] In addition to broadcasting and leafleting operations, USAF

also provided additional capabilities such as shows of force and harassing actions such as

---

[207]See Stanton, 237; U.S. Department of the Army, Army Concept Team in Vietnam (ACTIV), II-3.

[208]7th PSYOP Group, "Radio Broadcast Monitoring." Department of the Army, Pamphlet No. 525-7-2, *The Art and Science of Psychological Operations: Case Studies of Military Application,* vol 2 (Washington, DC: Government Printing Office, 1976), 534-536.

[209]U.S. Department of the Army, Army Concept Team in Vietnam (ACTIV), II-3, II-4.

[210]Chandler, 29-30.

sonic booms used for psychological effect.[211] PPM was also often integrated into major

bombing campaigns such as Rolling Thunder, Linebacker I, and Linebacker II.[212]

Smallest of the four key organizations was CORDS/POD, which was established

in 1967 and possessed a small cadre of PPM personnel. CORDS/POD was pivotal to the

overall PPM effort though.[213] CORDS itself was a large centralized civil-military

pacification organization established under military, MACV, control. Pacification or

Revolutionary Development (RD), though funded and often spearheaded by the US, was

a GVN program and responsibility. CORDS therefore did not control RD but advised

GVN provincial and district organizations on the program.[214] CORDS/POD likewise

supported GVN RD PSYOP efforts, usually at the provincial level. Being that RVN had

forty-four provinces and CORDS/POD so few advisors, CORDS/POD capabilities were

limited in providing support.

---

[211]Monro MacCloskey, *Alert the Fifth Force: Counterinsurgency, Unconventional Warfare, and Psychological Operations of the United States Air Force in Special Air Warfare* (New York: Richards Rosen Press, Inc., 1969), 132-136.

[212]Stephen T. Hosmer, *Psychological Effects of U.S. Air Operations in Four Wars 1941-1991, Lessons for Commanders* (Santa Monica, CA: RAND, 1996), 28-31, 35-40.

[213]Chandler, 239.

[214]Richard A. Hunt, *Pacification: The American Struggle for Vietnam's Hearts and Minds* (Oxford: Westview Press, 1995), 86-98.

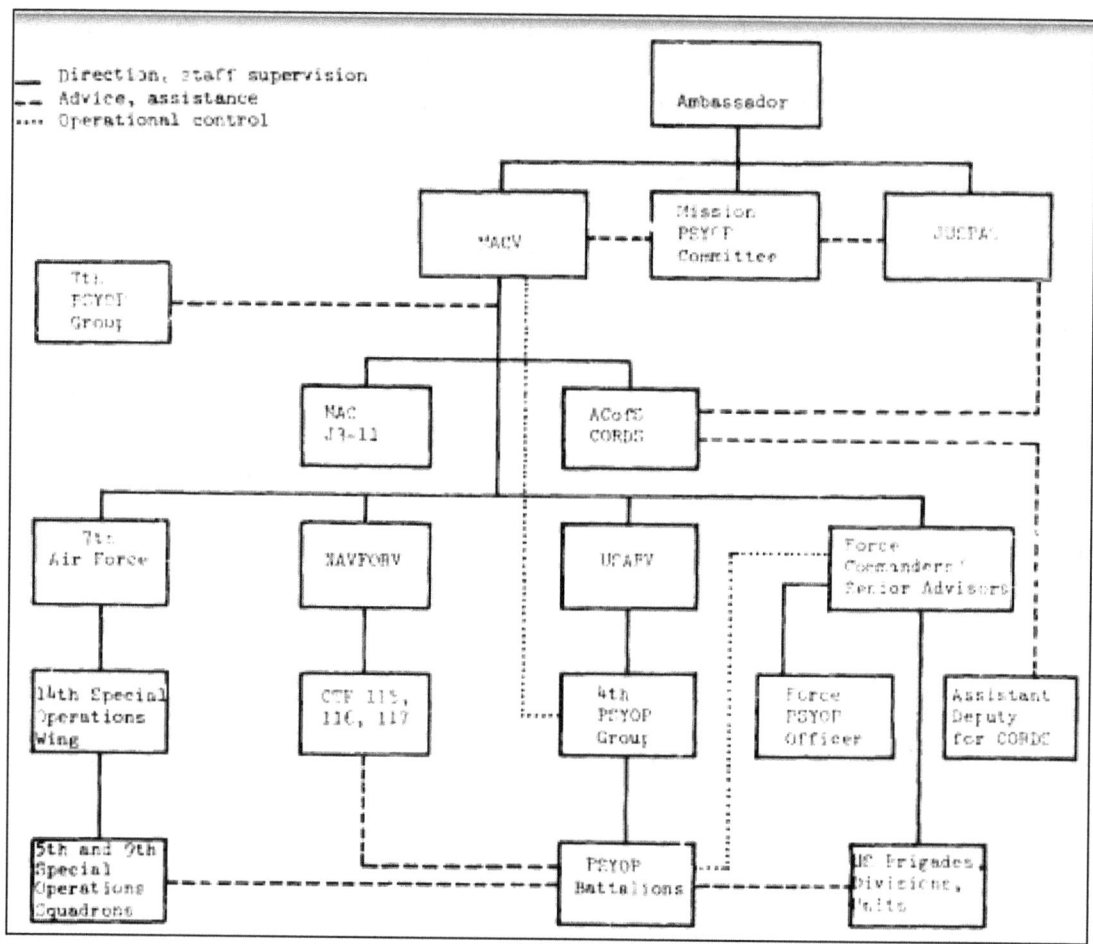

Figure 13. 1969 US PPM Command Structure
Source: U.S. Department of the Army, Army Concept Team in Vietnam (ACTIV), "Employment of US Psychological Operations Units in Vietnam," 7 July 1969, I-5.

Just as key, yet not under JUSPAO's directive authority, were the South Vietnamese peer organizations: the Vietnamese Information Service (VIS) and the ARVN Political Warfare (POLWAR) battalions. The VIS was the action arm of GVN's Ministry of Information; accordingly, it was the equivalent of the JUSPAO and partnered with it. Its focus mirrored the JUSPAO as well-strategic and national objectives, mostly using mass media dissemination vehicles. The POLWAR battalions though somewhat similar to US PSYOP battalions, were not a direct equivalent. As with the US PSYOP battalions, each CTZ had a POLWAR battalion; 10th POLWAR Bn (ARVN) in CTZ I, 20th POLWAR Bn (ARVN) in CTZ II, 30th POLWAR Bn (ARVN) in CTZ III, and 40th POLWAR Bn (ARVN) in CTZ IV.[215] The POLWAR battalions had a tactical mission similar to the US PSYOP battalions. PPM was not the only function of the POLWAR battalions, however. POLWAR battalions were also responsible for indoctrination of ARVN forces, social services for ARVN forces, and ARVN Post Exchange (PX) services. In effect, POLWAR battalions conducted influence operations internally and externally.[216]

---

[215]U.S. Department of the Army, Army Concept Team in Vietnam (ACTIV), II-3, II-4

[216]Jeffrey J. Clark, *Advice and Support: The Final Years, 1965-1973* (Washington, DC: United States Army Center of Military History, 1988), 29-31.

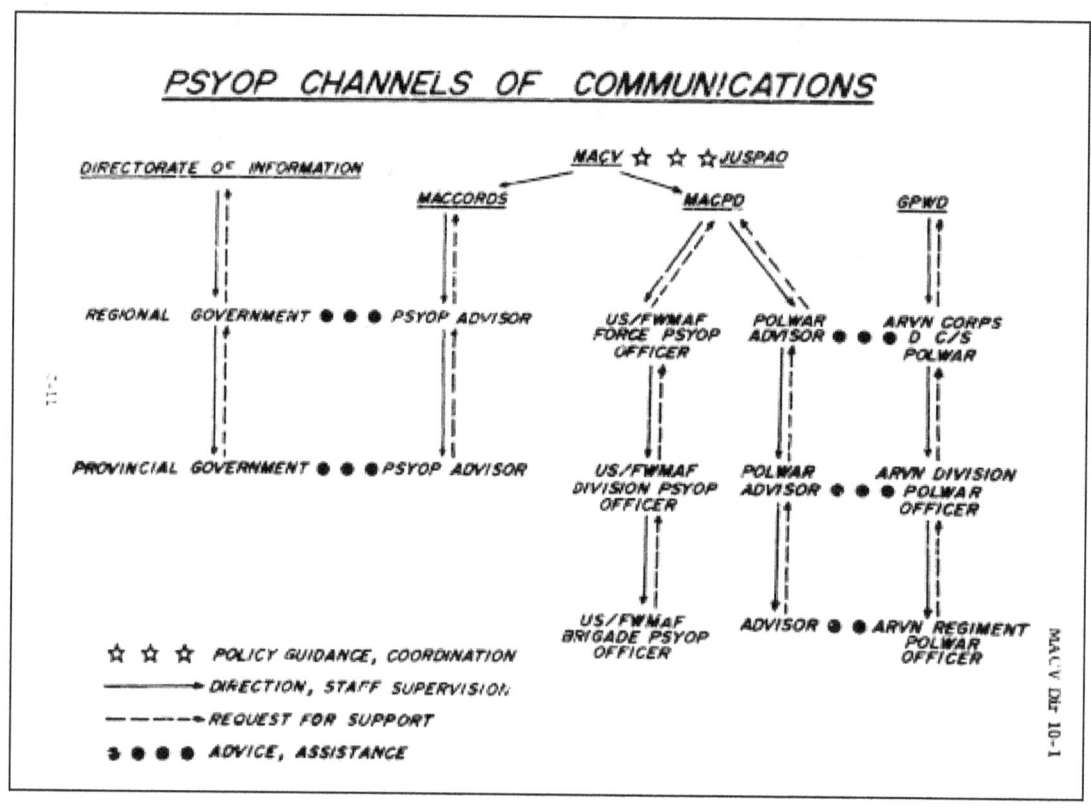

Figure 14. 1969 JUSPAO, MACV, and CORDS relationships
with Vietnamese peer organizations
Source: U.S. Department of the Army, Army Concept Team in Vietnam (ACTIV),
"Employment of US Psychological Operations Units in Vietnam," 7 July 1969, C-11.

PPM Priorities and Programs

The PPM organizational structure was complicated and PPM management was

equally as difficult. In order to best support operations and in accordance with its

mandate, JUSPAO provided guidance to the PPM organizations which was directive in

nature. Between 1965 and 1972, JUSPAO published over one hundred directives for

PPM organizations in order to integrate, synchronize, and prioritize efforts.[217] While

priorities shifted with circumstance, JUSPAO Policy Guidance # 51-published in

---

[217]Chandler, 277-282.

December 1967 which corresponded to the establishment of 4th POG in RVN, provides a good indicator of the cumulative PPM effort. The policy guidance directs the PSYOP priorities as:

1. The GVN Image
2. Chieu Hoi/Dai Doan Ket
3. Revolutionary Development
4. Refugee Program
5. Public Safety
6. US Image
7. GVN Mass Media Advisory Effort
8. Telling The Vietnam Story[218]

Though taken from a snapshot in time, the top three PPM priorities were enduring throughout the war and provide insight on what the US Ambassadors, Generals Westmoreland and Abrams, and the GVN wanted PSYOP to accomplish: promote the legitimacy, advantages, and achievements of GVN; encourage defection; and exploit pacification to gain the favor of the rural populace.

The GVN Image

The first JUSPAO priority, to improve "The GVN Image," was arguably the most difficult to accomplish. PSYOP assets were directed to assist "the GVN in projecting to the Vietnamese people a positive image worthy of full allegiance."[219] However, the desired image often suffered from the realities of the GVN being that, "the Vietnamese ruling establishment was dominated by the more educated elite, the new urban rich, and

---

[218]JUSPAO Planning Office, "Priorities in the PSYOP Effort." Department of the Army, Pamphlet No. 525-7-2, *The Art and Science of Psychological Operations: Case Studies of Military Application,* vol 1 (Washington, DC: Government Printing Office, 1976), 133-137.

[219]Ibid., 135.

the bourgeoisie left behind by the French. There was still inadequate concern for the

peasant and worker. In this respect the Viet Cong had a more revolutionary image

whatever their ultimate intentions."[220] To compensate for the situation and maintain

credibility, JUSPAO and MACV PPM programs accentuated the milestones of GVN

achievements while downplaying GVN shortcomings. The PPM efforts centered on

emphasizing the genuine democratic nature of the government, demonstrating military

success by RVNAF; highlighting civic and societal improvement programs, and

explaining populace and resource control measures.[221]

Paramount in garnering "full allegiance" of the South Vietnamese to the GVN

was establishing that the RVN was in fact a representative democracy. The first decade of

the GVN's existence suggested the opposite, producing only a lengthy despotism

followed by a series of military coups.[222] The period of 1955 to 1965 was plagued with

---

[220]Statement made by Ogden Williams during a RAND interview in 1971. Williams supervised AID and Chieu Hoi programs in the 1950s and 1960s. See J. A. Koch, *The Chieu Hoi Program in South Vietnam, 1963-1971* (Santa Monica, CA: RAND, 1973), 66.

[221]Department of the Army, Pamphlet No. 525-7-2, vol. 1, 133-137.

[222]In 1954, a provisional government was established South Vietnam with Emperor-in-exile, Bao Dai, appointing Ngo Dinh Diem as Prime Minister. The following year, among some controversy, Diem was declared the first president of the Republic of Vietnam. Diem was vehemently anti-communist but grew increasingly less popular with the South Vietnamese people and armed forces. Among other unpopular acts, Diem had replaced traditional village leadership with political appointees; suppressed opposing media organizations; forced rural population resettlements in Agrovilles and Strategic Hamlets; and brutally suppressed Buddhist, Cao Dai, and Hao Hao movements. Eventually he lost US backing and was assassinated in 1963 during a military coup led by General Duong Van Minh. A series of military coups followed. General Minh was overthrown by General Nguyen Khanh, and General Khanh was overthrown by Air Vice-Marshall Nguyen Cao Ky, who remained Prime Minister until the presidential election of 1967. Although a constituent assembly was elected and a national constitution drafted in 1966, the first twelve years of Vietnamese "democracy" was not so democratic. See

factional revolt, violent political suppression, corruption, nepotism, and assassination; all independent of the Viet Cong and DRV agitation also occurring. Finally, in 1966 and 1967, democratic processes produced local and national elected representative assemblies, an RVN constitution, and a legitimately elected president, President Nguyen Van Thieu. PPM assets reinforced the veracity of the democratic processes to assist the GVN in attaining credibility and soliciting popular commitment. JUSPAO handout #2309 and a "Preamble to the Constitution" leaflet illustrate the efforts.

 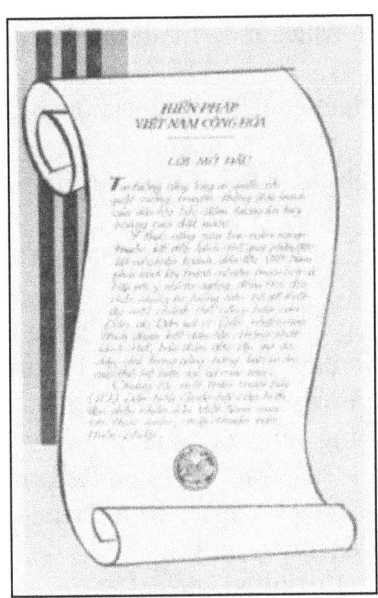

Figure 15. JUSPAO handout illustrating President Thieu's inaugural
address and JUSPAO "Preamble to the Constitution" leaflet

Source: Joint U.S. Public Affairs Office, Field Development Division. *National Catalog of PSYOPS Materials* (San Francisco, CA: JUSPAO, 1969).

Robert Thompson, "Vietnam: The clash between the Republic of South Vietnam and communist insurgents rapidly involved the worlds' greatest power in a war it could not win;" Thompson and Keegan, *War in Peace*, 181-183, 192-193; Phillips, 92, 154-156, 163-164, 203-206.

Second to emphasizing democratic reform was demonstrating RVNAF success in winning the war. To illustrate this, PPM forces were directed to "assist the GVN in exploiting ARVN victories, courage, and civic responsibility."[223] To enable and encourage the effort, JUSPAO Policy Number 68, Enhancement of RVNAF Image, was issued. Policy Number 68 provided specific guidance on the mediums and processes for exploiting RVNAF achievements, both to the civilian population for developing GVN support and to the RVNAF itself for improving morale. In particular, PPM organizations were directed to develop products "based on facts and achievements, rather than generalities which may fit all local situations."[224] General slogans, such as "ARVN is here to protect you," were questionable; whereas specific instances of military victories could be substantiated. A good example of this specificity is illustrated in the 10th POB leaflet number 10-1-68 highlighting a milestone victory of an ARVN unit:

> Long Phi 9/139 at Kien Phong Province
> Two days in a row, Nov. 17 through 19, 1967, the 9th Infantry Division launched the Long Phi 9/139 Operation, 10 km north of Kien Van district town aiming at wiping out what remains of the VC 502nd Bn. The VC were defeated seriously in the assault on Cao Lanh Reformed Training Center on Nov. 7, 1967.
> Our forces tangled with the enemy for two days. They caused heavy causalities to the enemy as follows"
>   -128 killed at front
>   -over 200 killed or wounded taken away by their friends
>   -2 captured
> Weapons seized by our troops:
>   -8 M3 sub-machine guns
>   -24 Russian built rifles
>   -1 M1
>   -3 flare-guns
>   -M7 Grenade launcher

---

[223] Department of the Army, Pamphlet No. 525-7-2, vol.1, 135.

[224] Joint U.S. Public Affairs Office. JUSPAO Policy Number 68, *Enhancement of RVNAF Image* (Saigon: JUSPAO Planning Office, 23 August 1968).

-1 57mm cannon tripod
-1 anti-aircraft machine gun sight
-7,000 electrical fuses
-38 rounds of ammunition for East German build machine gun
-120 57mm shells
-8 Thompsons
-3 East German build rifles
-1 M2 Carbine
-20 75 mm shells
-1,000 12.7 machine gun shells
-50 15 Kilo mines
-6,000 shells for East German built Machine Gun
-20 anti-tank shells
-250 flares
-3 loudspeakers
-82mm mortar sight
-90 81mm and 82mm shells
-10,000 K50 shells
-70 K40 shells
-15 anti-tank mines
-10,000 local grenades
-3 20 kilo explosive boxes
-2 40 kilo floating mines
-1,999 kilos of sulfur and gun powder
-5 Red Chinese built compasses

Gaining the good above mentioned success is because of the brave fighting spirit of the soldiers of the 9th Infantry Division, the Regional and Popular Forces and the contribution of the citizens. We won gloriously causing heavy damage to the enemy.

Believe in the authorities and the armed forces. If so we certainly will defeat the Communists.

Lastly, yet vital to enhancing the image of the GVN, was explaining the reasons behind GVN populace and resource control measures to the South Vietnamese people who often perceived the measures as nuisances. Populace and resource control measures are undertaken in a counterinsurgency effort to "provide security for the populace, deny personnel and material to the enemy, mobilize population and material resources, and to detect and reduce the effectiveness of enemy agents."[225] Population controls are activities

---

[225]Department of the Army, FM 1-02, 1-147.

such as curfews, travel restrictions, censuses, and identifications card issuance; resource controls are activities such as purchase limits, firearms controls, vehicle registrations, and trade restrictions.[226] The importance of explaining these measures was deemed so important that the JUSPAO issued guidance on specific measures such as the 1967 JUSPAO Policy Number 37, *National Identity Registration Program*, and the 1968 JUSPAO Policy Number 52, *PSYOP Aspects of the Public Safety Program (National Police)*. A good graphical and textual example of control measure explanations can be seen in JUSPAO Leaflet 1537 which stated:

The National Police serve the people by resources control.

Through their resources control teams the National Police protect the resources of the country and prevent them from being diverted into the hands of the enemy. More and more, the Viet Cong are being deprived of manpower, weapons, ammunition, and other essentials of war. Their combat capabilities have been considerably weakened, and their morale is being sapped.

To properly perform their duties the Police inspect cars, buses, boats, and other conveyances to prevent smuggling and infiltration. They check luggage, parcels, baskets, and boxes for illicit goods. They also conduct house-to-house searches in order to ferret out Viet Cong agents, hoodlums, and draft dodgers.

If you encounter minor difficulties because of inspections and searches please remember that the Police are protecting you and serving the cause of the GVN. Your cooperation is needed.[227]

---

[226]FM 3-24, 5-21; FM 3-24.2, 3-24 to 3-27.

[227]U.S. Public Affairs Office, Field Development Division, *National Catalog of PSYOPS Materials* (San Francisco, CA: JUSPAO, 1969).

Figure 16. JUSPAO Resources Control leaflet
Source: Joint U.S. Public Affairs Office, Field Development Division, *National Catalog of PSYOPS Materials* (San Francisco, CA: JUSPAO, 1969).

Chieu Hoi/Dai Doan Ket

The JUSPAO second priority, "Chieu Hoi/Dai Doan Ket," was the most recognized PPM support effort of the war yet one the most controversial. Chieu Hoi or "open arms" was the national amnesty program of the GVN that encouraged Viet Cong foot soldiers to surrender, defect, or "rally" to the government cause. Acting on advice from British and American advisors, the GVN initiated the Chieu Hoi program in 1963 as one arm of a comprehensive pacification campaign. Other key components of the campaign included resettlement projects, known as Strategic Hamlets, and National

Police and intelligence operations to capture or kill insurgents.[228] Chieu Hoi was different though. The premise of the Chieu Hoi program was that Viet Cong guerrillas could be persuaded to lay down their arms, receive political reeducation, and be reintegrated into South Vietnamese society. The political and military effect simultaneously strengthened the GVN and weakened the Viet Cong by shifting manpower from one side to the other.[229]

As pacification campaigns came and went, interest in the Chieu Hoi program grew and the program evolved. The program, initially managed by the Ministry of Psychological Warfare, was absorbed into the Ministry of Information in 1966, was rebranded as the Ministry of Information and Chieu Hoi (MICH) during 1968, and became a separate ministry in 1970. Along the way, Chieu Hoi program systematically established "reception centers" in provincial and district centers throughout the nation. At the reception centers, Hoi Chanh or "ralliers" were to receive medical treatment, housing, political reeducation, vocational training, and resettlement. Select Hoi Chanh were also given the opportunity to enter military, paramilitary, or governmental service.[230]

---

[228]Sir Robert Thompson, the British Military Advisor (BAM) and Rufus Phillips, chair of the CIA Rural Affairs Office, were instrumental in selling the idea of a repatriation program to South Vietnam's president, Ngo Dinh Diem. Based their experiences and understandings of counterinsurgency operations in Malaya and the Philippines, Thompson and Phillips provided Diem with the foundational pillars of his pacification program prior to Diem's assassination in November of 1963. The Chieu Hoi program, once established, endured through multiple South Vietnamese political administrations.

[229]Hunt, 21-25.

[230]Koch, 25, 73-88.

An offshoot of Chieu Hoi was Dai Doan Ket or the "National Reconciliation Program" (NRP). In 1967, Dai Doan Ket supplemented Chieu Hoi by expanding the target audience. In addition to Chieu Hoi's extension of amnesty, Dai Doan Ket included the guarantees of assistance in finding employment commensurate to previously held positions. In essence, Chieu Hoi appealed to the peasant Viet Cong while Dai Doan Ket targeted Viet Cong officers and Viet Cong professionals such as doctors.[231]

In addition to rallying people, an additional facet of Chieu Hoi was a weapons rewards program. As early as 1964, GVN paid additional bounties for Hoi Chanh

---

[231]Ibid., 36-39.

individual arms or for information regarding weapon caches. For Viet Cong guerrillas, who were often subsistence farmers, the weapons rewards were relatively substantial, especially for larger items such as crew served machine guns or mortars.[232]

Being GVN programs, Chieu Hoi, Dai Doan Ket and rewards for weapons, MACV did not administer them directly. Similar to the relationship CORDS had with Revolutionary Development, the US provided "support." US political, military, and economic support for Chieu Hoi grew steadily during 1965 and 1966; the creation of CORDS and a CORDS Chieu Hoi Division in 1967 though significantly improved the support relationship.[233] JUSPAO and MACV's PPM units also provided substantial support from their establishment as well, providing PPM advisors and direct operational assistance. The aim of the JUSPAO PPM support to Chieu Hoi was three-fold: to establish awareness of Chieu Hoi, to establish credibility for Chieu Hoi, and to fill its ranks by inducing Viet Cong to rally.[234]

Creating awareness of the Chieu Hoi program was national level responsibility conducted primarily using a combination of television and radio, and leafleting operations. By design JUSPAO and VIS undertook the mass media effort and MACV, supported by the USAF 14th Special Operations Wing, executed leafleting operations. The awareness drive was not inducement oriented or instructional but informational as is illustrated in JUSPAO Leaflet #1721:

---

[232]Ibid., 70-73.

[233]Ogden Williams was the first director of the CORDS Chieu Hoi Division. Williams was an experienced AID civil employee that had served in South Vietnam during the 1950s and 1960s. See Hunt, *Pacification*, 38; Koch, 26.

[234]Koch, 27, 60-69; Chandler, 91.

117

WHAT THE CHIEU HOI PROGRAM MEANS

The aim of the Chieu Hoi policy is to coordinate all efforts to create good conditions and favorable opportunities for the return of the mistaken elements of the community of our people, so that they may contribute to national reconstruction and assist in achieving social justice and freedom.

The Chieu Hoi policy is not a political trick. We need not resort to deceit, because we have been winning in all fields of military operations and through national reconstruction the living standards of the people have been greatly improved. The results so far obtained are concrete proof of our intentions.

The Chieu Hoi program is not a stratagem designed to cope with a particular situation; instead, the program is a continuing, national program which can help defeat the Communists and bring peace and democracy to our country. Through it our people can once again enjoy full happiness.

The Chieu Hoi policy is a policy of indulgence and generosity for the benefit of those persons who have gone the wrong way and who desire to return to the country and the people.[235]

To establish credibility for Chieu Hoi was more challenging. Potential ralliers had to be accessed by trustworthy sources that possessed firsthand knowledge of the program: the Hoi Chanh who had rallied. The Hoi Chanh were exploited to provide credibility in US and GVN psychological operations in two manners: broadcast and print products attesting to the validity Chieu Hoi program by Hoi Chanh and with face to face persuasion by Armed Propaganda Teams (APT) and Van Tac Vu or "Cultural Drama Teams" composed of Hoi Chanh.[236]

Broadcast and print products providing statements by Hoi Chanh attesting to the good treatment received upon rallying and to the reintroduction benefits of the program were widely disseminated. Where possible, photographs of the Hoi Chanh, specific Viet Cong military unit information, or specific regional information were included to

---

[235]Joint U.S. Public Affairs Office, Field Development Division, *National Catalog of PSYOPS Materials* (San Francisco, CA: JUSPAO, 1969).

[236]The Van Tac Vu were specialized members of the Armed Propaganda Teams that used music, songs, magic shows, storytelling, and theatrical performances to convey Chieu Hoi messages. Chandler, 33.

substantiate the authorship. In some tactical applications, Hoi Chanh even broadcast directly using loud speakers. The substance of credibility is illustrated in JUSPAO Leaflet #1927:

> Dear Friends,
> I am Huynh Thi Tan, alias "Ba Thanh," former Assistant Commander of the 558th Regional Company, operating in Tam Chau and An Phu, An Giang Province. I fought in the ranks with you before, but I have left for reasons which all of you must know.
> You, as well as I, have been fighting for many years, but our struggle has been exploited. We have been caught in the Communist propaganda net. They regard us as mere instruments, serving the Party's red ideology and imperialist ambitions. We have suffered all kinds of hardships and many of our friends have died shamefully for a meaningless cause. For us women, we have sacrificed the love of our families and children to serve the Party. We have suffered tremendously without any consolation.
> I made up my mind to leave the Viet Cong and return to the land of freedom with the assistance and leniency of the Government. I have found happiness and confidence in the future again. I sincerely hope that you, especially my fellow female cadre, will find an opportunity to rally to the National Cause. I know the Government and the people are always waiting for you.
> Hope to meet you again soon! Signed.[237]

Face to face persuasion of the APTs and Van Tac Vu was generally viewed as being the most effective means of establishing credibility-being village elders, families, and often Viet Cong guerrillas could speak directly with "former Viet Cong." In a 1972 RAND study of Chieu Hoi indicated that APTs "were invaluable in establishing the credibility and bona fides of the government, i.e., they were living proof that the government did not kill or mistreat the Viet Cong who rallied, despite Viet Cong rumors circulated by 'Radio Catinat'."[238] They also had a historical and cultural precedence. The technique originated with the Vietnamese Communist Party in 1944 and had been used

---

[237]Joint U.S. Public Affairs Office, *National Catalog of PSYOPS Materials.*

[238]Koch, 93.

119

by the Viet Minh and Viet Cong for twenty years before being adopted by the GVN.[239] Mimicking the communist approach, the RVN APTs and Van Tac Vu visited hamlets and villages throughout South Vietnam disseminating JUSPAO PPM materials and presenting Chieu Hoi messages in person.[240]

Just as Chieu Hoi evolved and expanded, the APT program grew with it transforming from two companies in 1964 to seventy five companies by its peak five years later. The program also migrated from the RVN MOI to the Ministry of Defense (MOD) the same year. As the program formalized, in-country doctrine was developed for APT use and the MACV 1969 *Armed Propaganda Team Handbook* was issued to units involved with the program. A good understanding of the tactical application of the APT was illustrated in the sample operations order found in the manual. A typical mission lasted several days and included rapport building, entertainment, and testimonials from Hoi Chanh. An excerpt from the manual demonstrates the sequence and pattern:

> Execution:
> a. Concept of the Operation. The operation be conducted in 6 phases over a seven day period.
> (1) Phase 1: Preparation, See Annex C (Operations Schedule)
> (2) Phase 2: Enroute, Establish CP
> (3) Phase 3: Distribution of Chieu Hoi psyops materials; group discussions, See Annex D (Psychological Operations)
> (4) Phase 4: Presentations by individual APT members; culture/drama team presentation, See Annex D.

---

[239]Ho Chi Minh established the first Armed Propaganda Team or *Doi Tuyen truyen Vo trang* of Vietnamese use in 1944 as the foundational element of the Indochinese Communist Party. Likewise, General Vo Nguyen Giap commanded the first communist propaganda brigade. Propaganda and indoctrination were the central keys to Ho Chi Minh's political and military philosophy. Not until 1964 did the GVN create similar organizations.

[240]Chandler, 82.

(5) Phase 5: Group discussions on GVN programs; presentations by individual APT members, See Annex D.
(6) Phase 6: Return to post.[241]

After awareness and credibility, the third aim of the JUSPAO PPM support effort for Chieu Hoi was to induce Viet Cong to "rally." The aim included two pivotal facets, persuading the Viet Cong to rally and providing a method for rallying. Rarely in either facet was "surrender" used; the actions of "surrendering" and "rallying" may have been the same but the sociological and psychological dimensions of rallying were determined to be more acceptable.[242] Also, as with awareness and credibility, a mix of conduits was used to reach the Viet Cong. Mass media, face to face operations, and leafleting, were all prevalent; however, leafleting was most prominent in terms of effort.

For persuading the Viet Cong to rally, in 1966 JUSPAO determined five major appeals for use in all inducement products and published them as directive guidance in the "The Chieu Hoi Inducement Program," JUSPAO Policy Number 16. The five major appeals were fear; hardships; loss of faith in the Communist victory; concern for family; and disillusionment. The most controversial of the appeals was "fear" which often manifested as graphic depictions of dead Viet Cong guerrillas in print products. The controversy though was not over the effectiveness of the appeal but rather that the use of graphic images reflected negatively on the GVN.[243] The appeals were inline though with a RAND study published the same year on Viet Cong motivations, and based on

---

[241]Chieu Hoi Directorate, Civil Operations and Rural Development Support (CORDS), Military Assistance Command Vietnam, *Armed Propaganda Team Handbook* (Saigon, 1969), 58.

[242]Chandler, *War of Ideas*, 40.

[243]Ibid., 44-69.

interviews of numerous rallied Viet Cong. The RAND study stated, "conditions most frequently cited as provoking their rallies were personal hardships, the poor economic conditions of the family, VC criticism or punishment, the risk of death, and homesickness."[244]

The second portion of inducement was supplying a method for rallying. "Method" products provided how-to instructions given to minimize the likelihood of the guerrilla being killed in the process of rallying. Also, to provide added reassurance Safe Conduct passes were promoted as official and legitimate documents that guaranteed the bearer humane treatment by military forces. Ironically, the credibility of safe conduct passes was so accepted that on occasion Viet Cong believed they could not rally without one.[245]

---

[244]J. M. Carrier and C. A. Thompson, Memorandum RM-4830-2-ISA/ARPA, *Viet Cong Motivation and Morale: The Special Case of Chieu Hoi* (Santa Monica, CA: RAND, 1966), 34.

[245]Chandler, 73.

In cumulatively reviewing the three aspects of Chieu Hoi PSYOP support-awareness, credibility, and inducement; two problems become apparent. The first difficulty is in determining cause and effect relationships between PSYOP stimuli and target audiences actions. A second difficulty arises in separating the effects of psychological operations supporting Chieu Hoi and the effects of the GVN controlled Chieu Hoi program itself. The two may or may not be separable. Qualitatively though, the level of awareness, creditability, and effectiveness of inducement are somewhat self apparent in that over the lifespan of the program almost two hundred thousand Viet Cong "rallied," the equivalent of twenty army divisions.

Revolutionary Development

The third JUSPAO priority, "Revolutionary Development," focused on the countryside of South Vietnam. Revolutionary Development (RD) was the title for the

GVN program and ministry created to bring the rural population under governmental

control. By bringing security to the countryside and improving socioeconomic conditions

of the rural peasantry, RD was intended to demonstrate governmental capacity; elicit

GVN allegiance; and correspondingly diminish Viet Cong support. Encompassing

political, economic, military, social, and psychological activities, RD was a multi-faceted

program employing a comprehensive approach to extend GVN authority.[246] Of note, RD

in general was also known as pacification, nation building, rural construction and the

other war, among other specific program titles.[247]

By the time of the US involvement in the late 1960s, RD consisted of several

programs collectively grouped under the term the New Model.[248] Programs and activities

included relocation of rural communities into fortified hamlet systems; educational and

vocational programs and school construction; establishment and support of local

governance bodies and facilities; sanitation, medical, and hygiene initiatives; and

agricultural enhancement programs introducing new strains of rice, improved fertilizer,

---

[246]Thomas W. Scoville, *Reorganizing for Pacification Support* (Washington, DC: Center of Military History United States Army, 1982), 3-4.

[247]Between 1955 and 1975 a number of pacification campaigns were conducted in South Vietnam. Most were similar in activity, such as resettlements and establishing local security forces, but varied in priority given and resources expended. Titles given of various efforts included *Operation National Security* in 1955, the Agroville Program in 1959, the Strategic Hamlet Program in 1961, the Will to Victory Program (Chien Thang) in 1964, the MACV led Victory Program (Hop Tac) in 1964, the New Model or New Life Program in 1967, and the Accelerated Pacification Campaign (Le Loi) in 1968. Various organizations oversaw the pacification programs, most notably the Vietnamese Ministry of Revolutionary Development established in 1965 and the MACV and AID conglomeration known as Civil Operations and Revolutionary Development Support (CORDS) established in 1967. Hunt, 11, 20-21, 25-30, 36, 88, 157.

[248]R. W. Komer, *Impact of Pacification on Insurgency in South Vietnam* (Santa Monica, CA: RAND, 1970), 2-5.

and motorized tillers. Based on the components, the New Model was essentially the continuation of previous pacification efforts although on a grander scale; according to the first director of CORDS, R. W. Komer, "the 1967-1970 program differs from its predecessors less in concept than in the comprehensive nature and massive scale of the effort undertaken, and in the unified management which pulled together the great variety of sub-programs carried out for the first time on a fully countrywide scale."[249]

To provide the scale, RD was largely funded and administratively overseen by US agencies; however, it was a GVN program.[250] Unlike other facets of the war, the "face" on RD programs and activities was "Vietnamese" and the bulk of the ground support working RD initiatives was indigenous. The support primarily manifested in three organizations: the RD Cadre Groups, the Regional Forces and Popular Forces (RF/PF), and the National Police. The RD Cadre Groups were the core of the RD program. The mobile 59-man groups visited hamlets for extended periods organizing village "self defense" forces, establishing local governance bodies, facilitating socioeconomic development, and conducting psychological operations. The RF/PF paramilitaries were also key and provided regional and district security along roadways and other infrastructure. Lastly, the National Police dealt with identifying and combating Viet Cong Infrastructure (VCI).[251]

---

[249]Ibid., 3.

[250]Hunt, 11-15, 68, 82.

[251]William C. Westmoreland, "Report on Operations in South Vietnam, January 1964-June 1968." William C. Westmoreland and U.S.G. Sharp, *Report on the War in Vietnam (As of 30 June 1968)* (Washington, DC: U.S. Government Printing Office, 1968), 231-232.

To assist in exploiting the RD program and help generate the intended results, JUSPAO and CORDS/POD assets were directed to "bring RD activities and successes to the attention of the rural people at whom the program is directed with particular emphasis on publicizing the rewards of self-help to hamlet and village dwellers."[252] The directive required a similar approach to those used in improving GVN image: explaining the reasons behind programs and accentuating the benefits, while downplaying undesirable aspects. The undesirable aspects of RD were especially difficult to mitigate as relocation programs were frequently imposed rather than offered and were usually culturally undesirable.[253] Likewise, even when rural security improved notably from late 1968 to 1970, fear and intimidation of Viet Cong reprisals remained.[254] PSYOP assets therefore focused on awareness and benefits, as also illustrated in the 1968 MACV *Handbook for Military Support of Pacification*:

> Psychological operations are directed at the people in the area as well as at the enemy. Whether the people be initially friendly, uncommitted or hostile toward the government, the objective of PSYOPS—as of all RD—is to persuade the people to support the GVN. To this end, disciplined, well behaved troops showing friendly, sincere interest in the people and respect for individual rights and prosperity will have the most favorable impact on the local people. PSYOPS themes will include explanations of why troops are in the area and what RD can do for the people by their cooperating with the GVN. Against the enemy, the

---

[252]Department of the Army, Pamphlet No. 525-7-2, vol 1, 135.

[253]The Vietnamese inhabitants of rural villages were at times forcibly relocated into Agrovilles, Strategic Hamlets, and New Life Hamlets, after which their existing homes and villages were burnt down in order to keep them from returning. Also, the majority of Vietnamese, regardless of religious orientation, practiced the cultural norm of "ancestor worship" which created deep ties between families and the lands where their ancestors were buried. As a result of the forced resettlement and cultural insensitivity, many resettled Vietnamese were highly disillusioned with the hamlet programs. See Elliot, 407; Phillips, 143.

[254]Chandler, 156-157; Phillips, 270-271.

PSYOPS objective is to persuade the individual soldier to stop supporting the enemy cause and to rally to the GVN through Chieu Hoi and Doan Ket programs. Hence, PSYOPS themes will stress the positive benefits of RD and sow doubt about the justice of an enemy cause that opposes RD.[255]

For the most part, the tangible positive benefits of RD were the New Life Development programs available at the hamlets. New Life Development programs included Education and Culture, Hygiene Sanitation, Land Reform, Agricultural and Animal Husbandry, Cooperatives, and Public Works.[256] These programs were mostly administered by the RD Cadre Groups, who by design were also the influence conduit to the rural populace. Using PSYOP material provided to the Provincial RD Cadre Group Psychological Warfare Section, the RD Cadre Groups performed face to face communication similar to the APTs. To support the RD Cadre Groups, JUSPAO provided a weekly RD newspaper, *Viet-Nam Ngay Nay* [Vietnam Today], and a monthly RD magazine, *Houng Que* [Rural Spirit]; each promoted RD programs and provided interesting success stories. When available, *Van Tac Tu* [Cultural Drama Teams] were also incorporated into RD Cadre efforts. While entertaining the hamlet residents, the Van Tac Tu also reinforced the GVN message. Specific handbills were also provided to the RD Cadre Teams as required to promote the specific programs, self defense forces, or social issues of hamlet life; as here JUSPAO Handout #2368, outlines the eleven objectives for *Ap Doi Moi* [New Life Hamlets].[257]

---

[255]Military Assistance Command Vietnam, *Handbook for Military Support of Pacification* (San Francisco, CA: 1968), 9-10.

[256]Ibid., 18.

[257]By 1967, three categories of hamlets were established relative to the degree of GVN control exerted: the *Ap Doi Moi* [Real New Life Hamlet], *Ap Binh Dinh* [Pacification Hamlet], and *Ap Tan Sinh* [New Life Hamlet] Real New Life Hamlets were

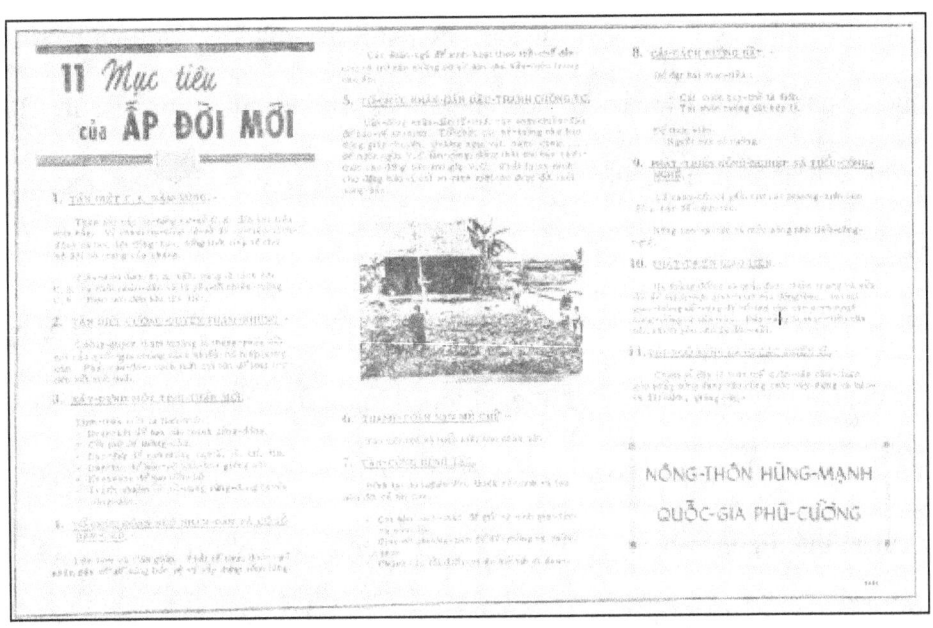

Figure 20. JUSPAO Handout #2368 providing eleven hamlet objectives

Source: Joint U.S. Public Affairs Office, Field Development Division, *National Catalog of PSYOPS Materials* (San Francisco, CA: JUSPAO, 1969).

The RD Cadre Group efforts were intensive and prolonged events. At times, more temporary measures were required to boost RD efforts in a specific area. These temporary RD measures were called Hamlet Festivals, Go Teams, and County Fairs. The temporary measures were cordon and search operations coupled with civic and psychological operations, in general "all include the cordoning of the hamlet selected for the operation, a search of the hamlet by GVN forces, and finally, conduct of PPM for the

designed for development, Pacification Hamlets were in the process of construction and development, and New Life Hamlets were constructed and developed in accordance with the established six point criteria (census taken, self defense forces established, hamlet defense system established, liaison and logistics system organized, social organization established, and hamlet government elected). Military Assistance Command Vietnam, *Handbook for Military Support of Pacification*, Annex A.

128

purpose of evidencing GVN concern for the people of the area."[258] Hamlet Festivals, Go Teams, and County Fairs, were combined operations with both US forces and RF/PFs or National Police though and therefore counteracted to a degree the primary psychological aim of RD.[259]

PSYOP also supported another RD effort geared more specifically in bringing security to the countryside although not mentioned in the JUSPAO policies. The effort was called the Phung Hoang (Phoenix) program. Phung Hoang, though originating with the US Central Intelligence Agency (CIA), was a Vietnamese effort and integral in RD. The program utilized select RF/PFs, the Special Branch of the National Police, the Vietnamese Central Intelligence Organization, and other Vietnamese assets such as Provincial Reconnaissance Units (PRUs) to "indentify and root out the secret Communist apparatus within South Vietnam, the so-called Viet Cong Infrastructure, or VCI."[260] In essence, Phung Hoang was a human intelligence (HUMINT) and direct action (DA) program aimed at neutralizing intermediate and higher ranking VCI leaders and facilitators.[261]

The processes and activities of the Phung Hoang program were tremendously varied. Typically, information collected from Chieu Hoi ralliers, paid informants,

---

[258]Military Assistance Command Vietnam, *Handbook for Military Support of Pacification*, 50.

[259]Ibid., Annex B.

[260]William E. Colby and Peter Forbath, *Honorable Men: My life in the CIA* (New York: Simon and Schuster, 1978), 266, 269-270; Hunt, 116, 153.

[261]Under Phong Hoang, VCI were categorized into three groups: A-leaders and formal party members, B-cadre and holders of responsible jobs, and C-rank and file Viet Cong. Phong Hoang efforts focused on A and B level VCI. Colby, 268.

interrogations of enemy prisoners of war (EPW), or Vietnamese children was provided to

intelligence centers, such as Intelligence and Operations Coordination Centers (IOCC) or

Police Interrogation Centers (PIC), which compiled, analyzed, and verified the

information.[262] If meeting certain criteria, which also varied, actionable intelligence was

provided to an appropriate civil or military organization that attempted to capture or kill

the VCI. Numerous "action" agencies were involved in capturing or killing the VCI

members, PRUs--advised by US Navy SEALs, often were the most active.[263]

Most of the US support, and the associated PPM support, for Phung Hoang came

from CORDS. Established in 1968, the "Phoenix Office" of CORDS consisted of a

handful of CIA and MACV advisors that provided guidance, coordination, and support at

national, provincial, and some district levels.[264] The CORDS PPM support for Phung

Hoang focused on one objective-enabling HUMINT. To encourage and facilitate

HUMINT collection, PPM was used to promote awareness of information gathering

campaigns such as the Popular Information Program and Hamlet Information Program; to

publically identify known and suspected VCI members and solicit information regarding

them; and to convey methods for and the importance of reporting VCI.[265]

---

[262]Various titles and acronyms existed for various intelligence and operations centers. In general, military Information and Operations Coordination Centers (IOCC) included district level centers (DIOCC) and provincial level centers (PIOCC). Civil or police interrogation centers included district and provincial level centers, as well as National Police Interrogation Centers (NPIC). Valentine, 79, 80, 131, 230.

[263]Valentine, 160, 230.

[264]Hunt, 153-154.

[265]Valentine, 283-284.

PPM assets, US and Vietnamese, promoted awareness of the information programs using face to face methods and a variety of broadcast and print means. Specific products for enabling VCI identification and methods of reporting primarily consisted of two items; "Wanted Posters" and a Phung Hoang comic book (see Annex B). Although sounding simplistic, the two products significantly contributed to HUMINT collection.[266]

When VCI members were indentified, posters or handouts containing their names or photographs could be created (see figure 22). The products were then posted in local areas with appeals for the specific VCI members to rally and for members of the community, including families, to provide information on their whereabouts. To maximize the print effort, local village chiefs and hamlet leaders were sometimes leveraged, through encouragement or pressure, to bring additional emphasis to the local community. Print products were also reinforced with by portable or aerial loudspeaker broadcasts likewise calling specific VCI members by name. The violent reputation of the PRU itself also increased pressure on named VCI members to rally rather than be tracked down; as being pictured a Phung Hoang wanted poster meant the person was on the "black list."[267]

[266]Colby, 282-284.

[267]Colby, 273; Valentine, 282-283.

To augment the "specific" wanted posters, the "general" Phung Hoang comic book was created. Similar in concept to the Chieu Hoi Safe Conduct Pass, the Phung Hoang comic book provided the method for peasants and villagers to report information concerning VCI activity, and how to do it anonymously. The comic book pictographically and textually conveyed the intent of Phung Hoang posters, leaflets, and broadcasts and how villagers could act on the information.[268]

Collectively, the task of supporting Revolutionary Development with psychological operations was likely the most difficult task of all based on diversity of operations, the number of psychological operators allocated, and the lack of direct

---

[268]The entire Phong Hoang comic book can be found in Valentines' *The Phoenix Program* and in Appendix D of this study. Valentine, 283, Appendix A.

control. From accentuating the benefits of New Life Development programs to inducing villagers to report on neighboring villagers suspected of communist activities, the spectrum of activity was extraordinarily broad. Oddly, overseeing this broad spectrum was only a handful of advisors working in CORDS/POD and the CORDS Phoenix Office. Heavily dependent on the JUSPAO and the MACV 4th POG for material support and acting almost exclusively through Vietnamese civil and military assets, RD PPM was administratively and organizationally challenging. The outcome of all the PPM effort though shares the fate of the RD program itself, it undoubtedly contributed to the higher effort yet pacification was never achieved.

Tactical PPM

Apart from the JUSPAO priorities, PPM was employed extensively in support of tactical military operations in Vietnam.[269] Tactical PPM support focused on achieving short term psychological results to support select aspects of military operations; more specifically tactical PPM was "employed to prevent civilian interference with military operations, to exploit individual susceptibilities and weaken the will to fight, and finally, when warranted by the tactical situation, to induce the enemy to surrender."[270] The means used to attain these results were mainly truck-mounted or man-portable loudspeakers, aerial loudspeakers, and leafleting operations used or coordinated by three- man PPM

---

[269]The tactical level of war is defined as "the level of war at which battles and engagements are planned and executed to accomplish military objectives assigned to tactical units or task forces." Tactical PSYOP support therefore deals with the psychological operations conducted to directly support the tactical missions of military units. FM 1-02, 1-182.

[270]Department of the Army, Field Manual (FM) 33-1, *Psychological Operations U.S. Army Doctrine* (Washington, DC: Government Printing Office, 1968), 7-3.

teams. Each of the four US PSYOP battalions and four ARVN POLWAR battalions provided PPM teams in direct or area support to maneuver units.[271]

Preventing civilian interference with military operations was a primary responsibility of mobile PPM teams and unique to tactical operations. Preventing civilian interference was, as it is today, predominately conducted using loudspeaker broadcasts to inform the civilian populace of military operations and to provide directions to them.[272] The loudspeaker broadcasts were usually conducted as an integrated portion during cordon and search operations.[273] At times leafleting operations were also used preemptively to mitigate civilian casualties and damage to civilian property.

Most of the tactical weaken the will to fight and induce the enemy to surrender procedures mirrored the previously mentioned Chieu Hoi and Revolutionary Development efforts. Although at the tactical level, two novel PSYOP techniques were developed to assist in short term military goals, Quick Reaction Requests (R) and Earlyword. QRs were time-sensitive leaflet drops or taped messages for loudspeaker broadcasts conducted within twenty-four to seventy-two hours of the request. Normally,

---

[271]US PSYOP battalions doctrinally possessed Light Mobile Operations Teams (Team HA) which facilitated the mobile support of Loudspeaker Operations (Team HB) and Audiovisual Operations (Team HE). Audiovisual teams more often provided pacification support and loudspeaker teams more often provided support to combat operations. ARVN POLWAR battalions possessed similar mobile teams. See Department of the Army, Army Concept Team in Vietnam (ACTIV), III-4, B-4, H-1 to H-6; Jeffrey J. Clark, *The U.S. Army in Vietnam, Advice and Support: The Final Years, 1965-1973* (Washington, DC: United States Army Center of Military History, 1988), 30-31; Stanton, 237-238.

[272]FM 33-1, 7-4.

[273]Department of the Army, Army Concept Team in Vietnam (ACTIV), B-4; Bernard W. Rogers, *Cedar Falls-Junction City: A Turning Point* (Washington, DC: U.S. Government Printing Office, 1974), 37.

QRs were used to exploit recent ralliers using personalized themes, such as specific names and Viet Cong units. The second technique, Earlyword, was an even more rapid exploitation means and both a technical device and a tactic. Earlyword was a communications adapter which when fitted in loudspeaker equipped special operations aircraft, allowed the aircraft intercom system to connect directly to a loudspeaker bypassing the requirement for prerecorded messages. Using the device, ralliers could be used to convey messages directly to the battlefield.[274]

How thoroughly these techniques and tactical PPM were employed in support of maneuver operations is difficult to measure. PPM support and integration was limited by the relatively small number of tactical PPM troops available, especially prior to 4th POG expansion in 1968. However, several notable examples of tactical PPM support exist during major combat operations such as during Operation Irving, Operation Geronimo II, and Operations Cedar Falls.

An important instance of tactical PPM limiting civilian interference and enabling maneuver options occurred during Operation Irving. The operation was conducted during 1966 in the RVN province of Binh Dinh, located along the south central coast. The combined US, RVN, and South Korean operation was intended to remove the Viet Cong forces and political structure from the heavily populated coastal region. During one battle in the operation, a hamlet with a large Viet Cong presence, Hoa Hoi, was blocked and cordoned by a US cavalry unit. A heli-borne PPM team then conducted a loudspeaker broadcast directing the villagers to leave the hamlet and the Viet Cong to lay down their

---

[274]Department of the Army, Army Concept Team in Vietnam (ACTIV), B-4, I-10, G-7.

arms. Though no ralliers manifested, approximately two hundred villagers came out of the hamlet leaving only Viet Cong remaining. With all non-combatants removed, the hamlet was pummeled with eight hundred rounds of 105mm high explosive artillery and AC-47 gunship fires prior to being assaulted the following day. Apart from saving the lives of the civilians, the PPM technique facilitated a greater array of lethal options to the maneuver force, inevitably saving US lives during the assault.[275]

A similar example of tactical PPM inducing the enemy to surrender occurred the same year in the neighboring province of Phu Yen during Operation Geronimo II. After a day of fighting, a US airborne infantry battalion had enveloped the remnants of a Viet Cong battalion. A three-man tactical PPM loudspeaker team then was employed and "convinced thirty-five enemy soldiers to surrender." The remainder of the Viet Cong were then assaulted and overrun. In effect, the employment of the tactical PSYOP team removed a platoon sized element from the battle, greatly reducing the size of the force being opposed during the assault and saving US lives.[276]

Aside from the particular instances, Operation Cedar Falls offers an indicator of how tactical PPM cumulatively affected combat operations. Operation Cedar Falls took place during early 1967 in the Cu Chi Province of South Vietnam just north of the capitol, Saigon. Clearing the known Viet Cong stronghold, known as the Iron Triangle, was the goal of the operation and to do so required the largest single effort of the war.

---

[275]John M. Carland, *The U.S. Army in Vietnam, Stemming the Tide, May 1965 to October 1966* (Washington, DC: United States Army Center of Military History, 2000), 262-269.

[276]George L. MacGarrigle, *United States Army in Vietnam, Taking the Offensive, October 1966 to October 1967* (Washington, DC: United States Army Center of Military History, 1998), 81-82.

The operation was comprehensive in nature with wide hammer and anvil style tactics directed at the Viet Cong; destruction of extensive Viet Cong underground complexes; massive population resettlement and the destruction of villages; and intensive defoliation operations.[277]

One of the uncharacteristic results of the nineteen day operation was the unusually large number of Viet Cong ralliers; in fact almost as many Viet Cong rallied as were killed in action--540 rallied and 750 were killed. The high percentage of ralliers was certainly an aspect of the nature of the operation but tactical PPM significantly contributed to process. During the operation, tactical PPM elements used QR leafleting with personal appeals and general leafleting with fear appeals but with specific instructions on where to how and where to rally. The combination proved effective. One QR leaflet dropped during the operation illustrates the personalized appeal read:

> To my dear friends still in the VC ranks, I am Le Van Sa, medic of the medical team of VH (MB3011). I followed the VC and their false inducement. I found fault with our people and nation. I have gone the wrong way. I have rallied to the GVN and have been warmly welcomed, well treated. At the present time I am very happy at the CH (Chieu Hoi) Center. I also saw my family who are living in the Resettlement Center of GVN. I send to you this letter so that you too could rally to the Government side where you can start a new life and see your families. My dear friends: Hung, Rong, Tieng, Chi, Tu Dan, Minh Nhan, Tha Luong, Tam Thu, Thanh, Huyen, Lion, Thau, Mong Tieng, Ut and Gan, all of you should return to GVN as soon as possible. Staying with VC, you will have no place to hide. You can use any Chieu Hoi leaflet and take the nearest road to report to the GVN or Allied Military Installations. You will be treated as we are now. There are more than 300 VC who have returned to the Nation Just Cause in a very short time. They are having a good living here at the CH Center. They have been well treated. My dear friends you should rally right now to avoid useless deaths. Tet is going come very soon. Rally to reunite with your families. The door of the Chieu Hoi Center is wide open for your return.[278]

---

[277]Rogers, 19, 23-24, 61-66, 71-72, 79.

[278]Ibid., 56-57, 74-76, 79.

Tactical PPM support throughout the war varied greatly by method, emphasis, and zone. However, the basic three facets of tactical PSYOP support--civilian noninterference, discouragement, and surrender, were applied extensively and produced results. In any of the cases where effects were demonstrated, PSYOP was certainly not the only factor that caused to the outcome. Yet tactical PSYOP did contribute to the outcome and provided the method for achieving it.

PPM Summary: The Vietnam War

The "American War" portion of the Second Indochina War was unsuccessful. The effort did not prevent the collapse of the RVN or avert the associated consequences of the domino theory, as Laos and Cambodia both fell prey to communist aggression in 1975. However, this does not mean that MACV's COIN operation was unsuccessful. A number of external factors, most arguably on the American "home front," contributed to the outcome. Inside of the COIN operation, however, the successfulness of the PPM campaign remains debatable.

When viewed through the lens of the classic counterinsurgent PPM synthesis derived in chapter 3, the PPM of the Vietnam War did address all of the classic counterinsurgents' aims and principles. Yet some aspects were more successful than others. The classic counterinsurgent's primary aim of swaying "the population to support the government over the insurgent" was the same as JUSPAO's stated top priority, the "GVN Image." Massive efforts were applied to garnering the allegiance of the people to the government through PPM and, during the later years, civic action. In the end though, the GVN could not overcome its image as a "western puppet" and a despotic government.

The government, plagued with corruption and dominated by urban dwelling French and English speaking elites, failed to sell itself to the rural majority.

Several of the classic counterinsurgent principles were successful, however. The reconciliation efforts of the Chieu Hoi program, though not solely a PPM function, did remove the equivalent of twenty enemy divisions from the battlefield. Effects were also realized in the Propaganda of Deed effort conducted by CORDS and Vietnamese RD ministry during 1968 to 1970. Although the rural Vietnamese may not have favored the GVN, they did see tangible effects of its governance. Also, PPM did enable HUMINT through the Phung Hoang program.

Two other principles though were more questionable, that of the use of civilian run PPM agencies and uncovering the veiled aims of the insurgents. Although JUSPAO did operate throughout the war and prioritize and synchronize efforts, it would have not been possible without the established of the "boots on ground" 4th and 7th Pugs, the ARVN POLWAR Battalions, and the Special Operations Air Force support. The civilian JUSPAO was mass media oriented in a land where the majority of the population lived without electricity. The primary means to accessing the population was leaflet, loudspeaker, and face to face communication, none of which were within JUSPAO's capabilities. Lastly, though many attempts were made to uncover the veiled aims of the Viet Cong, the true aims of the Viet Cong and the DRV were likely not realized until 1975 when the reeducation programs started.

According to the classic counterinsurgents views, the PPM in Vietnam was focused on the correct principles and some did produce the desired results, yet comprehensively failed to achieve the primary aim. PPM efforts in Reconciliation,

Propaganda of Deed, and, enabling HUMINT all contributed to the campaign. However, the credibility of the GVN was never established; therefore, the primary PPM task was not achieved.

CHAPTER 6

CONCLUSIONS AND RECOMMENDATIONS

Psychological warfare does not fit readily into familiar concepts of war. Military science owes much of its precision and definiteness to its dealing with a well defined subject, the application of organized lawful violence. The officer or soldier can usually undertake his task of applying mass violence with having to determine upon the enemy. The opening of war, recognition of neutrals, listing of enemies, proclamation of peace—such problems are considered political, and outside the responsibility of the soldier. Even in the application of force short of war, the soldier proceeds only when the character of the military operations is prescribed by higher (that is, political) authorities, and after the enemies are defined by lawful and authoritative command. In one field only, psychological warfare, is there endless uncertainty as the very nature of the operation.

— Paul M. A. Linebarger, *Psychological Warfare*

Conclusion

This thesis examined the origins of twentieth century US Psychological Warfare, Psychological Operations, and Military Information Support Operations (PPM); the emphasis placed on PPM in US COIN doctrine; the synthesized views of four classic counterinsurgents; and two PPM case studies. The aim of the thesis was to accomplish one overarching objective: to demonstrate that effective PPM is vital to success in countering insurgencies. Concepts discussed in the Conclusions and Recommendations section are derived from and supported by the research and focused on the singular objective. Although subject to interpretation, the thesis suggests the emphasis placed on PPM in COIN has eroded and a number of lessons can be drawn from past PPM applications.

All attempts have to been made to quantify and substantiate conclusions when possible; however, due to the nature of the subject matter, that is not always possible. Psychological Warfare, Psychological Operations, and Military Information Support

141

Operations deal with human beings, and human nature is often fickle and subjective. Although subjective, in the terms of the material covered, the four established fundamental PPM and COIN questions are answered as follows.

Is PPM Essential for Successful COIN?

All four chapters of this thesis indicate that PPM is not only essential in COIN but may hold some degree of primacy among the pillars (military, paramilitary, political, economic, psychological, and civic). Not that the "psychological" facet is, in any way, independent of the other factors but PPM enables and exploits each of the factors. PPM supports and exploits military and paramilitary operations and is crucial in enabling intelligence collection which drives operations. Likewise, PPM exploits the political, economic, and civic actions to maximize effects.

The examination of the evolution of PPM and COIN doctrine suggests that early US Army doctrine writers considered PPM essential in COIN. From the original 1951 COIN manual FM 31-20, *Operations Against Guerrilla Forces* onward, PPM has been integrally included as a core factor. In fact, FM 33-5, *Psychological Operations* (1962) was the first US Army manual to use the term counterinsurgency. However, the emphasis placed on PPM in COIN has varied over the years (see figures 1 and 2). The observed pattern is that although PPM emphasis has ebbed and flowed, a downward trend in emphasis has occurred. Doctrine written during the Vietnam War included the greatest degree of emphasis, while doctrine written during our current conflicts includes only vague references placed without context. It appears that PPM, previously a core tenet in US COIN doctrine, has become intentionally or haphazardly less doctrinally relevant.

Also examined was the literature and theories of four classic counterinsurgents to determine if PPM was essential in their views. Each of the four wrote extensively on PPM and deemed it vital if not paramount in countering insurgencies. If fact both Robert Thompson and Edward Lansdale devoted chapters to PPM in their most widely read works, *Defeating Communist Insurgency* and *In the Midst of Wars*. Although each addressed PPM differently, ranging from "hearts and minds" to "dirty tricks," all had witnessed the effects of PPM firsthand in their insurgency experiences and considered PPM vital. Frank Kitson was especially convinced of requirement for PPM in countering insurgencies stating, "the main characteristic which distinguishes campaigns of insurgency from other forms of war is that they are primarily concerned with the struggle for men's minds."[279]

Similarly, when the COIN campaigns of two radically different cases studies were examined, both studies indicate PPM as essential. The Dhofar Rebellion in Oman and the Vietnam War ended with dramatically different results yet PPM was key in each. Dhofar and Vietnam demonstrate how interventionist and host nation forces used PPM to achieve milestone results such as evidenced in reconciliation programs and intelligence gathering. Another indicator of essentialness can be observed relative to the primary aim of each. PPM in the Dhofar Rebellion primarily sought to "persuade the population of the integrity of the Sultan's government" while in the Vietnam War the primary aim intended to improve the "GVN Image." In Dhofar, though it took a coup and five years of combat, the population was persuaded and the campaign ended successfully. In Vietnam, after twenty-one years of fighting, the "GVN Image" remained less than credible and the

---

[279]Kitson, *Bunch of Five*, 282.

campaign ended unsuccessfully. Of course, this is only one factor in a myriad of thousands that affected the campaigns; however, it is an indicator of the value of PPM's essentialness.

Based on four areas of research: doctrinal emphasis, opinions of classic counterinsurgents, and two disparate case studies, effective PPM is an essential element in COIN. The writers of nascent US Army doctrine considered PPM important enough to include its teachings in every manual. Each of the classic counterinsurgents included PPM theory in their writings. Also both case studies indicated PPM's vitality in the overall success of a COIN campaign.

COIN and PPM: Best Practices?

When addressing what PPM practices have been historically beneficial it must be noted that effects are based on circumstance. Although a practice may have produced results in a particular application, similar results may not be reproduced in a different setting. For enabling military operations in COIN and promoting loyalty to a government, three key practices are validated in this research, both in the writings of the classic counterinsurgents and the case studies. Although many interesting and effective practices were identified, three were consistently proven: (1) persuading insurgents to change sides; (2) demonstrating governance by propaganda of deed; and (3) utilizing PPM to enable intelligence operations.

Persuading insurgents to change sides, whether to "come-over" as in Dhofar or to "rally" as in Vietnam, is key in an insurgency for three reasons. First, since insurgent manpower is drawn from the population, it decreases the manpower available to the insurgents. Second, properly "reconciled" former insurgents often become agents of

144

propaganda for the government and thus attest the legitimacy of the government such as Vietnam's Armed Propaganda Teams. Third, former insurgents are valuable sources of background and contact information, which, once extracted, facilitates further military operations. Major General Tony Jeapes' following statement clearly demonstrates this phenomenon: "Then, too, by killing him you merely deprive the enemy of one soldier. If he is persuaded to join the Government forces the enemy again become one less, but the Government forces become one more, a gain of plus two."[280]

Tactically this process has two facets: (1) inducing the defection and (2) enabling the defection. To persuade or coerce insurgents to "reconcile" or "rally" is extremely complicated requiring significant target audience analysis. Based on the circumstances, appeals may be hard or soft, such as fear of death or longing to be reunited with a loved one. Attaining credibility for the offered reconciliation program is best gained through personal testimonials of former insurgents, such as Vietnams' Hoi Chanhs. Often the appeal or PPM provided stimuli are not the overwhelming argument to cause defection but rather accentuates existing desires. Likewise, defections must be enabled. Historically, defections have been successfully aided by "safe conduct passes." Safe conduct passes or similar items add an additional level of credibility to potential defectors and offer reassurances of humane, responsible treatment.

Demonstrating governance by Propaganda of Deed is likewise a best practice. Although not a primary PPM function, it essential that PPM exploit Propaganda of Deed. In each studied case, whether Dhofar or Vietnam, or any of the classic counterinsurgents' domains, it is apparent that insurgencies are developed by agitators who exploit existing

---

[280] Jeapes, *SAS Secret War*, 39.

governmental grievances. Whether economic, political, or social, grievances exist in all governments and not all can be remedied. What is vital in COIN is identifying those grievances being exploited by agitators and addressing them to invalidate an insurgent movement. The grievances could be economic disenfranchisement such as land ownership in Malaya; or political such as democratic corruption experienced in the Philippines; or social such as ethnic and religious discrimination in Iraq and Afghanistan. Once identified and addressed, even if not rectified, PPM must exploit milestone tangible successes so the population can touch, taste, and see benefits derived from the government. Propaganda of Deed thus becomes the manifestation of the relation between the government and the people.

The third best practice calls for using PPM to enable intelligence collection, more specifically HUMINT. The enabling collection takes two forms; one is general and one specific. The first relates in general to promotion of security and governance. When a population perceives an established governmental authority and marginalizes fear of reprisal, the number of people willing to provide information to security forces increases. Of course PPM cannot provide this security but rather enhances and exploits security. The second form of enabling is more directly a result of PPM: inducing and enabling information gathering such as rewards for information programs. Inducing often manifests in providing a motive for potential informants to report information in exchange for a benefit such as financial reward, esteem, or the removal of a threat. The enabling portion requires providing a method to conduct the act while maintaining a guarantee of anonymity to the informant. Specific methods are countless but in Dhofar, "letter boxes" were used for cold drops, and in Vietnam, Phung Hoang "wanted posters" included phone numbers to police centers. Today, numerous electronic means are available and even less personal risk is required from an informant.

As observed in the writings of classic counterinsurgents and case studies, various PPM practices have been employed. Some traditional methods produced few effects while some less traditional methods produced great effects –all dependent upon relative circumstances. The three primary best practices derived in this research were the "reconciliation," "deed," and "HUMINT" practices.

COIN and PPM: Doctrinal Relationship Lost?

The observed COIN PPM "lessons lost" primarily revolves around doctrine. As COIN and PPM doctrine evolved over the last fifty years, their close association has grown farther apart. Naturally, COIN is not the only operation that PPM supports and PPM is not the only facet worth considering in COIN; however, the two are inextricably linked. And yet, the current US Army COIN manuals, FM 3-24, *Counterinsurgency* and FM 3-24.2, *Tactics in Counterinsurgency,* and the current US Army PPM manuals, FM 3-05.301, *Psychological Operations Process, Tactics, Techniques, and Procedures* and FM 3-05.302, *Tactical Psychological Operations Tactics, Techniques, and Procedures* have lost what their predecessors possessed (see figure 1 and 2). In fact, the Vietnam era "Counterguerrilla" and "Psychological Operations" manuals demonstrated the relationship more succinctly and emphasized in volume and in detail the role PPM serves in COIN.

Worth mentioning, the 1966 version of FM 33-5, *Psychological Operations Techniques and Procedures* provided a full chapter on detailed PPM support to COIN (See Annex A). The manual contained a comprehensive view of the soft and hard side of

PPM ranging from Nation Building Programs to Counterguerrilla Operations while also addressing PPM support of Population and Resources Control and countering Subversive Propaganda Organizations. The manual not only provided emphasis on COIN but also detail on how to support the tenets of COIN. Similarly, the 1963 FM 31-22, U.S. *Army Counterinsurgency Forces* and 1967 FM 31-16, *Counterguerrilla Operations* each contain far more thorough discussion on purpose of PPM and integration than do current manuals. Though the newer manuals contain jargon about Information Engagement and Information Operations, they lack substantive insight, background, and method.

COIN and PPM: Doctrine Not Explored?

What is missing in current COIN PPM? While the current doctrine deficit includes "lessons lost" from previous manuals, current doctrine also fails to take the innovative next steps to harness the full capability of PPM. Of note on the "lessons lost," many of the previously addressed pacification genre "lessons lost" from the 1966 FM 33-5 pertain directly to the Essential Services, Governance, and Economic terminology used in FM 3-24. Likewise, PPM support to COIN Intelligence previously discussed is lacking as well. What has not been addressed previously is the greater detail and emphasis FM 3-24 and FM 3-24.2 provides on the insurgent organizations, characterizing them as Movement Leaders, Combatants (Guerrillas), Political Cadre (Underground), Auxiliaries, and the Mass Base.[281] Although this description is not new, it was likely ignored in the past as it often is currently. In fact earlier US Army publications address insurgent organizations in similar terms. The 1967 FM 31-16, *Counterguerrilla Operations*

---

[281]Department of the Army, FM 3-24, 1-11; Department of the Army, FM 3-24.2, 2-3.

acknowledges guerrilla organizations are composed of "combat, combat support, and combat service support organizations and military organizers and advisors, and civilian political, economic, and psychological organizers."[282] yet it appears no emphasis on targeting the full array of the tiers existed. In the classic counterinsurgents' works, and in the Dhofar and Vietnam case studies, insurgents were predominately viewed as "leaders" or "soldiers" and targeted by PPM accordingly. No mention was found in any study that expanded on the concept.

Many of the classic counterinsurgents addressed separating guerrillas from leaders and the population from the insurgents. In fact even FM 3-24.2 emphasizes two of the three directed PSYOP message to the insurgents: (1) "Divide insurgent leaders and guerillas," and (2) "Divide insurgents and mass base," yet no thought is given to how PPM can influence other components of the insurgent organization.

What must also be addressed is an emphasis on targeting the political cadre and auxiliaries to separate or neutralize the capability they provide. Though not nearly as visible as the leaders and combatants, the political cadre and auxiliaries are intermediaries that maintain an insurgent organization. The FM 3-24 defines the political cadre and auxiliaries as follows:

> Political Cadre. The cadre forms the political core of the insurgency. They are actively engaged in the struggle to accomplish the insurgent goals. They may also be designated as a formal party to signify their political importance. The cadre implement guidance and procedures provided by the movement leaders. Modern non-communist insurgencies rarely, if ever, use the term "cadre"; however, these movements usually include a group that performs similar functions. Additionally, movements based on religious extremism usually include religious and spiritual advisors among their cadre.

---

[282]Department of the Army, FM 31-16, 22.

Auxiliaries. Auxiliaries are active sympathizers who provide important support services. They do not participate in combat operations. Auxiliaries do the following:

- Run safe houses.
- Store weapons and supplies.
- Act as couriers.
- Provide passive intelligence collection.
- Give early warning of counterinsurgent movements.
- Provide funding from lawful and unlawful sources.
- Provide forged or stolen documents and access or introductions to potential supporters.

Since the political cadre and auxiliaries are often semi-legitimate citizens and participate in society, efforts to "rally" them may not be effective. However, pressure can be applied to disengage them from activities that support insurgent organizations or at least degrade the support provided. Influencing cadre and auxiliaries is a difficult task but can be accomplished if intelligence and circumstance allow. Especially susceptible are those cadre and auxiliaries who perform a public service or require travel or commerce in the conduct of their support. Cadre such as political officers (spiritual advisors), recruiters, financiers, and propagandists; and auxiliaries such as couriers and logistical "mules" fit in this category.

The capability of political officers or spiritual advisors to provide support to an insurgent group may be degraded or neutralized if circumstances permit. For instance, Kitson's advice of uncovering the "veiled aims" of insurgent groups can be applied to individuals or subgroups.[283] In modern terms, this tactic might be likened to the "character assassination" methods seen in political races. If a cadre member or subgroup's status in the insurgent organization requires upholding moral codes,

---

[283]Kitson, *Low Intensity Operations*, 84-85.

philosophical disposition, or the conduct of "good works," failure to maintain behavioral norms may degrade established authority and thus lessen effectiveness. Of note, key in the process of character assassination or highlighting "veiled aims" is specificity. Just as the JUSPAO recommended using "facts and achievements, rather than generalities" in building up the RVNAF image; claims that can be substantiated work equally as well for degrading an image.[284] When circumstances permit, concepts such as uncovering the "veiled aims" can be applied in detail and lessen the capability of a political cadre member or group to execute their role.

A similar concept can be applied to insurgent recruiters. Recruiters may solicit potential recruits with a variety of appeals such as esteem building, social responsibility, nationalism, ethnic hatreds, religious duty, or financial incentives. Recruitment appeals, once identified, may be combated in detail through the use of a counterargument delivered by a credible personality or group, such as the GVN Hoi Chanh. Also, the recruiter may be personally attacked by illustrating examples of deceit, personal cowardice, vice, selfish motivation, etc., where specific examples exist. Whether attacking the appeal or the recruiter, insurgent recruitment may be degraded.

Likewise, insurgent financiers and financial support may be offset by illustrating examples of financial mismanagement or misuse. Charitable donations and "taxation" often fund and supply insurgent organizations. By highlighting discrepancies between advertized intentions and the actual of use funds or material support, some support may be withheld. Of course, this applies more towards donations than forcible taxation and varies with circumstance. As with the previous political cadre, if the donation or taxation

---

[284]Joint U.S. Public Affairs Office, JUSPAO Policy Number 68.

system cannot be effectively attacked, the financier or tax collector may be attacked as a group or individual highlighting excess, extravagance, or misuse where applicable. Figure 22 illustrates a Vietnam era PPM attack on Viet Cong taxation of rice, indicating the rice as being consumed by the traditional Vietnamese enemy, the Chinese.

Of the political cadre, no effort is more overt than that of the propagandist. Traditionally, whether Huk or Taliban, propaganda efforts are relatively centralized in themes, products, and methods. By examining a sufficient quantity of insurgent propaganda, core psychological objectives can be extrapolated and targeted in general or in detail. General targeting involves attacking fundamental contradictions or undesirable aspects of an insurgent program, as in the Marxist-Communist agenda of the adoo. Though espousing the slogan "Dhofar for the Dhofaris," the adoo sought to impose a communism system which was contrary to the native tribal system and religious practices. In return, the Sultanate's Information Services adopted the slogan "Islam is our Way, Freedom is our Aim." The Sultan's slogan highlighted the distinctive feature between the two forms of governmental and attacked the communist program in general, degrading its effectiveness.[285] Propagandists can also be attacked in detail by illustrating exaggeration, discrepancies, or deceit in specific instances, degrading the credibility of insurgent propaganda. No historical example better demonstrates a detailed PPM attack than the case of Nguyen Ban Be. Be, a Viet Cong ammunition bearer, was captured during a small attack by ARVN forces in 1966. Not knowing his fate, Viet Cong propagandists assumed he had been killed along with his companions and selected for a "hero emulation" propaganda campaign. A fictitious account of Be's final stand was widely circulated, and Be became well known across the RVN. Once it was discovered that Be was alive, RVN and US PPM forces exploited the situation, and gave Be a massive amount of publicity. The attack in detail, supported with photographic evidence, discredited the "hero emulation" campaign and the Viet Cong propaganda apparatus.[286]

---

[285]Jeapes, 26-27, 38, 60, 133.

[286]Chandler, 139-145.

Lastly, auxiliaries are the most difficult to target as their activities are minimal in scope and often are coerced. If the situation merits though, auxiliaries may be induced to cease support to insurgents or lessen the amount or kind of support provided. Performing functions such as transporting or caching war materials or providing sanctuary, auxiliaries can be inundated with knowledge of governmental penalties for aiding insurgents. More specifically, auxiliaries can be made aware of risk and danger brought into their own homes and to their own families as a result of insurgent support. Being that auxiliaries are generally less committed to an insurgency than combatants or political cadre, when properly stimulated, they can play a vital role in breaking an insurgent chain of support.

Apart from political cadre and auxiliaries, an additional aspect that has not been recognized is Edward Lansdale's sixty year old concept of Shepherding. Lansdale effectively employed the technique at tactical and strategic levels to influence political and military circumstances during insurgencies. To be effective, intelligence and circumstance must exist to support it but Lansdale did induce insurgents to leave an area through creative PPM and also drew them into areas where they could be targeted. He also applied the concept to non-combatant populations causing villages to move of their own initiative in the Philippines and convincing Vietnamese Catholics to resettle as well.[287]

Recommendations

Taking into account lessons learned from Dhofar and Vietnam as well as Iraq and Afghanistan, PPM practitioners must to continue to progress and refine the strategies and tactics for supporting COIN operations. In particular, a training and operations focus must be integrated in COIN doctrine and operations not in general but in detail and with contextual purpose. In addition to the "lessons lost" of Vietnam era doctrine which provided specific PPM guidelines in Nation Building, Environmental Improvement Programs, and Population and Resource Control Measures; and the classic counterinsurgents' thoughts on how PPM supports HUMINT; a step forward must to be taken to effectively combat all tiers of insurgent organizations. While breaking the link between insurgent leaders and the guerrilla combatants and between the insurgent organizations and the mass base remains crucial; attacking the political cadre and auxiliaries is an equally important and indirect method to degrade insurgent operations.

What is absolutely essential in the big picture is that counterinsurgency practitioners understand the nature of the conflict they engage in. Insurgency and counterinsurgency are not primarily military struggles but rather battles of wits where

---

[287]Lansdale, 72-73.

patience, narrative, and allegiance are the determining factors. People cannot be killed into allegiance but given patience and the proper narrative, allegiance can be attained and insurgency defeated. PPM is the military commander's essential tool for this problem.

GLOSSARY

Agitation. Incitement, an appeal for action. It is based on the existence of a grievance, am impelling situation, or the occurrence, often by design, of a dramatic or atrocious incident.

Armed Propaganda Team. A team made up of Vietnamese ralliers under the Chieu Hoi program. Members of the Armed Propaganda Team were selected from ex-Hoi Chanh and are given training in face-to-face psychological operations procedures.

Counter-psychological operations. Actions taken to detect and counteract hostile psychological activities.

Counterinsurgency. Those military, paramilitary, political, economic, psychological, and civic actions taken by a government to defeat insurgency.

Counterpropaganda. Programs of products and actions designed to nullify propaganda or mitigate its effects.

Counterterrorism. Offensive measures taken to prevent, deter, and respond to terrorism.

Guerrilla Warfare. Military and paramilitary operations conducted in enemy-held or hostile territory by irregular, predominately indigenous forces.

Insurgency. An organized movement aimed at the overthrow of a constituted government through the use of subversion and armed conflict.

Propaganda. Any form of communication in support of national objectives designed to influence the opinions, emotions, attitudes, or behavior of any group in order to benefit the sponsor, either directly or indirectly.

Psychological Operations. Planned operations to convey selected information and indicators to foreign audiences to influence their emotions, motives, objective reasoning, and ultimately the behavior of foreign governments, organizations, groups, and individuals. The purpose of psychological operations is to induce or reinforce foreign attitudes and behavior favorable to the originator's objectives.

Psychological Warfare. The planned use of propaganda and other psychological actions having the primary purpose of influencing the opinions, emotions, attitudes, and behavior of hostile foreign groups in such a way as to support the achievement of national objectives.

Special Operations. Operations conducted by specially organized, trained, and equipped military and paramilitary forces to achieve, military, political, economic, or informational objectives by unconventional military means in hostile, denied, or politically sensitive areas. These operations are conducted across the full range of military operations, independently or in coordination with operations of conventional, non-special operations forces. Political-military considerations frequently shape special operations, requiring clandestine, covert, or low visibility techniques and oversight at the national level. Special operations differ from conventional operations in degree of physical and political risk, operation techniques, mode of employment, independence from friendly support, and dependence on detailed operational intelligence and indigenous assets.

Subversion. Action designed to undermine the military, economic, psychological, or political strength or morale of a regime.

Target audience. An individual or group selected for influence or attack by means of psychological operations.

Target audience analysis. The process by which potential target audiences are identified and analyzed for effectiveness, accessibility, and susceptibility.

Terrorism. The calculated use of unlawful violence or threat of unlawful violence to inculcate fear; intend to coerce or intimidate governments or societies in the pursuit of goals that are generally political, religious, or idealogical.

Unconventional Warfare. A broad spectrum of military and paramilitary operations, normally of long duration, predominately conducted by indigenous or surrogate forces who are organized, trained, equipped, supported, and directed in varying degrees by an external source. It includes guerilla warfare and other direct offensive, low visibility, covert, or clandestine operations, as well as the indirect activities of subversion, sabotage, intelligence activities, and evasion and escape.

APPENDIX A

Excerpt from FM 33-5, Psychological Operations Techniques and Procedures (1966)

CHAPTER 4

PSYCHOLOGICAL OPERATIONS IN COUNTERING INSURGENCY

Section I. CHARACTERISTICS OF PSYCHOLOGICAL OPERATIONS IN AN INSURGENT ENVIRONMENT

38. General

Counterinsurgent operations consist of military, political, social, economic, and psychological actions undertaken by the local government to modify and ultimately eliminate the root causes of insurgency; accomplished through the development and modernization of the country as well as the development of a participant society.

39. Supplementary Instrument of National Power

·In an insurgent environment, the elements of national power are normally fully committed. It is natural, therefore, to find operations being conducted to change the attitudes, emotions, opinions, and behavior of the population, the government establishment, and the insurgents. Specific psychological operations are conducted to cause the planned changes desired by the government. These operations do not replace current political, economic, and military operations but are blended into them to optimize the likelihood of government success. An example of such an operation is the amnesty program which encourages defection. Military intelligence gains cooperative sources of information; the military doesn't have to kill or rout out these individuals; the police can register and maintain surveillance over defectors; and the government has an opportunity to show its friendship and sincerity to

everyone in the nation through its treatment of these persons. The amnesty program relies heavily on the contrast between a secure life and the shadowy, hunted life of an insurgent facing a continuous threat on his life. The program would not work without such contrast.

40. Insurgency and Unconventional Warfare

Although psychological operations may be effectively integrated to support military actions in limited and general warfare, it is essential to success in both counterinsurgency and unconventional warfare. An insurgency, whether or not it is subversive and externally directed and assisted, occurs only where there are economic, social, and political environments which breed discontent. It is apparent, then, that any long-lasting solution will require more than tacit approval of government policies. This environment of discontent is sought by subversive agencies; and they base their attempts to establish broad, mass, organizational support for insurgency upon these seed-beds of incipient or latent insurgency. Not only must appropriate and sincere governmental actions be taken to eliminate such sources of discontent, but appropriate psychological campaigns must be energetically pursued to deny the insurgent his base of support, to give the nation a sense of unity of purpose, and to justify restrictive and repressive control measures taken during counterguerrilla operations.

Section II. SUPPORT OF NATIONAL INTERNAL DEFENSE AND NATION-BUILDING PROGRAMS

41. General

No tactical counterinsurgent program can be effective for long without major, nation-building programs. To build support for a legal, nontotalitarian government, the government must be worthy of that support. Thus, any solution to the insurgency must satisfy the political demands of the insurgency. For this reason, military actions and psychological operations must be subordinate to the political sphere and its short- and long-range demands. The nation undergoing the stresses of a subversive insurgency must develop a plan which will include security as well as development, for there must be environmental improvement along with the measures for population and resources control and counterguerrilla operations.

42. The Nation-Building Programs

a. General. Nation-building programs take a variety of forms; and psychological operations play a vital role in every aspect of all the programs by building morale, engendering cohesive group feelings, assisting civic action, and creating and disseminating informational programs: in short, selling the programs by word and deed to the local population.

b. Support. All persons associated with the government establishment are, in effect, propagandists and good-will ambassadors for the national program. They must be made to accept this responsibility or the programs will be futile. After all, insurgency is a negative reaction to government, and governmental employees and representatives must help prove the government's honorable intentions through their own conduct. The people must be convinced that the government is not just to be tolerated, but that it is to be desired and is worth supporting with labor, intelligence, taxes, and the many other forms of cooperation which create stability.

c. Need for Developing National Unity. Nationalism, even if developed before national independence is gained does not automatically guarantee the degree of national unity essential to the functioning of a modern nation-state. The spirit of nationalism and the struggle for independence often creates an illusory sense of national unity. Once independence is achieved, however, the old ethnic, linguistic, religious, tribal, clan, and regional loyalties reassert themselves. The most disruptive divisions appear wherever large racial minorities perform key economic roles. Additionally,

these developing societies may have highly trained cosmopolitan intellectuals at one extreme and peasants and tribal members at the other end of the value systems. Under these straining social and economic conditions, the role of individuals and groups, as participants in these societies, is often under-valued and misunderstood. Strong and effective states are important; but to defeat an insurgency, power should be widely shared among groups throughout the society. Governments which cannot gain and maintain the support of major groups within their country and cannot satisfy physical and psychological needs by putting these groups to work on constructive tasks will, in the long-run be insecure and vulnerable to violent overthrow. Thus, nation-building is not only a matter of economic development, but a bond of unity must be developed between the people and the government. National unity may be developed by the programs suggested below. National ethos and pride must also be developed. Deep-rooted, spontaneous patriotism comes only after generations of interaction and with the development of a commonality of interests and values.

d. Psychological Objectives Which Develop National Unity. Any strong, united group has a quality which we call spirit, esprit de corps, elan, or morale. This feeling about the group is shared by the group's members. It is an intangible, a pride, a camaraderie, and an emotional attachment or cohesion which gives strength and meaning to the group and its members. By establishing programs which emphasize the psychological objectives, by stressing group participation activities, one can develop national unity.

(1) *Realistic, worthwhile goals.* Groups must satisfy some of man's wants. Group membership must reap rewards for efforts expended, and these goals must be of graduated importance based upon the effort required to achieve the reward. To illustrate, rewards may be graduated from "thanks" to a Medal of Honor. For the majority of persons, rewards should be frequently and easily achieved. Long-range, economic goals are desirable; however, a wage increase for

governmental employees or a needed bridge over a river is more readily translated into a positive reaction than would a hydroelectric power project which would take 15 years to complete. This long-range project would have to be broken down into numerous stages or hurdles to achieve the desired sense of accomplishment necessary in developing national unity.

(2) *Sense of prestige.* Man wants recognition of his merit and acknowledgement of his efforts in the group's behalf. The desired sense of prestige is derived from those members of the group that the individual most wants to impress. An individual does not necessarily want to impress a nation, but he does want to impress people within that nation who are important to him. In a developing nation, this is often limited to the family, the extended family, the clan, or the tribe. Even though the local leader of the man's family were the primary source of prestige, one would strive to integrate national and local programs so that slowly, over the course of time, the national government will become a source of prestige similar to that in most modern, nation-states. To illustrate further, an individual might not give his life for a government; but he would give it for his wife or family because of his close and continual interaction with all the members of this primary, functional group. Failure or lack of willingness to commit himself would destroy his sense of prestige and would likely result in his elimination from the group.

(3) *Sense of belonging.* Membership in a group must provide emotional rewards. Men gain a sense of satisfaction and security from belonging to strong, cohesive groups. Entertainers, religious leaders, and politicians all recognize the value and emotional response associated with collective activity. Group singing, football rallies, and political gatherings are often so emotionally stimulating that the persons in attendance attempt over and over again to relive the experience. This can be seen in the alumni attending football games and then going down into the locker room "just to talk to the boys," or in the proliferation of veterans organizations after every war where the members can talk about old times and be with "old friends." To develop national unity, an individual must feel this sense of belonging to something to which he can contribute and in which he can participate. The individual must be assured that his union, or unit, or group, with his consent, knowledge or information, worked with other groups to achieve national goals, and that he shared his goals and that he was rewarded for his part in achieving them.

(4) *Sense of equity.* Perhaps nothing is more destructive to group morale than inequitable treatment within the group. An individual should get a reward for his efforts, and it may contribute to the group, but unless he feels that he is getting his share of the privileges and responsibilities, he will resent it. There should be a proper reflection of the contribution of the individual, no more and no less. In education, welfare, community affairs, etc., there must be agreement on the reasons for the differences in treatment. It is recognized that there will be differences; however, the differences should be justifiable.

(5) *Understanding the situation.* A key psychological objective in an insurgency is to keep everyone informed of what the government programs are and how all of the parts of the society fit into the national plans. The unknown can create fear and anxiety. In response to these feelings, people search for "explanations" for their situation in terms of their wants. This

often leads to over-simplification which places the government in a bad light and destroys unity; therefore, it is essential that a thorough informational program be instituted with timeliness, honesty, and sincerity as cornerstones. This interest in keeping the people informed will generate faith and respect as well as contribute to the sense of belonging.

(6) *Trend towards success.* A group which has worked together successfully in the past is led to expect success in the future. Thus, realistic emphasis on national successes will enhance national unity through the people's desire to be on a "winning team." In a political world, no one wants to associate with a loser, thus the long-range plans and programs must reflect positive attitudes and goals. In this program it is essential to assure that the current government will be in office long after the subversive insurgent efforts are defeated and the disillusioned are brought back into the nation as participant members.

(7) *Sense of purpose.* A high purpose, such as supporting the national government through the trials and tribulations of everyday life, is important in developing national unity. Groups under pressure need a cause to justify and inspire their efforts and sacrifices during an insurgency. The cause or purpose must have an emotional appeal because most people under pressure tend to follow their emotions. To achieve an appropriate sense of purpose which will appeal to men with differing interests, the constitution, charter, or laws must be broad enough to permit local and regional leaders to live within its bounds, yet still to its sense of purpose. A nation's policies and long-range objectives should be stated so that the people will know why it would be desirable to live with this governing body rather than with the subversive

"government" which is also attempting to win the allegiance of the people.

43. Psychological Operations Support of Environmental Improvement Programs

a. Purpose. An environmental improvement program is designed to develop faith and confidence in the legally constituted government of the country where counterinsurgent operations are taking place. This program must stimulate cooperation and support among appropriate segments of the population. The degree of cooperation and support from the civil population will reflect their attitudes toward the government. Environmental improvements should involve constructive programs designed to restore or give the civil community a condition of normalcy and a manner of daily living which will eradicate, or at least diminish, the causes for disaffection and insurgency. Unfortunately, these programs must be justified as well as implemented to insure popular support, for improvement does not mean the same thing to all peoples. To illustrate, a hydroelectric power plant is recognized as being nationally desirable when it will provide jobs and services for thousands. However, when a dam must be built upstream, flooding the river banks which have been tribal homes for centuries, these people will not necessarily see the hydroelectric plant as desirable. To retain these people as willing participants in the society, the desirable and necessary feaures of both the project and the displacement must be thoroughly and convincingly sold to the leaders and opinion formers of the affected tribes. Similarly, a new, straight, hard-surfaced road may be desired to decrease motor maintenance and improve speed and efficiency of transporation in an area; but merchants and towns to be by-passed must be convinced of the necessity and desirability of this new road which will decrease their businesses. Inequities and injustices must be recompensed or they will show the government's lack of sincere interest in the welfare of the people.

b. Planning. During the incipient or latent stages of an insurgency, the majority of the country's psychological operations efforts should be directed towards the support of environmental improvement programs. Such programs as military civic action, economic de-

162

velopmental programs, and political and social improvement programs should receive the majority of the propaganda efforts. Population and resources control and counterguerrilla operations programs should receive subdued propaganda programs, with emphasis on planning and training requirements. At the national level, the programs are prepared and designed primarily to nullify the basic causes of disaffection among segments of the civil population. These programs will normally include political, economic, social, military, and psychological actions in an operational area. Plans and programs in each area must be constantly reviewed and evaluated. These programs take a variety of forms. They may include governmental and legal reform, community relations activities to stimulate exchange of ideas, civic action, development of local resources, improvement of agricultural and manufacturing techniques, improving health conditions, expansion of educational facilities, and troop information to instill a social conscience.

c. *Method.* Psychological operations should be used in environmental improvement programs by—

    (1) Disseminating information concerning the proposed plans for economic, political, and social improvement.

    (2) Re-educating the population through mass media, as well as by rendering a community service by publishing and broadcasting news and directives.

    (3) Exposing the causes of disaffection which are manufactured and fallacious; in short, counterpropaganda. (Insurgent groups may have conducted such an active propaganda campaign that the people can no longer recognize and distinguish between real and imagined needs.)

    (4) Building and reinforcing morale of the population, military as well as civilian.

    (5) Pointing out to the civil sector the efforts of the military in assisting them in building needed schools, community projects, and the like. (This action underscores the cooperation of the military and civilians in working toward common goals.)

d. *Need.* Psychological operations is the instrument through which national and community goals and their interrelationships are explained. Without an extensive psychological operations program necessary cooperation for the total counterinsurgent program cannot be obtained.

e. *Reinforcement.* The government and its supporting agencies are critical determinants of the government's "image" in the minds of the people. The armed forces are particularly important because of their close contact with the people; consequently, they can help create a favorable image of the government. The favorable impact of civic action must be reinforced and spread by the psychological operations explanation of what the army, as a part of the government, is doing. Without this propaganda reinforcement, the value and contribution of military civic action may remain localized and not be widely understood in its role of developing national unity and actively showing the national government's genuine interest in the people and in the solution of their problems.

44. Psychological Operations Support of Population and Resources Control Programs

The guerrilla must be separated from his source of support; this support lies within the local population. Thus, a primary target for psychological operations is this local, civilian population. Direct appeal to the guerrilla, who may be a fanatic during this accelerating phase of insurgency, may net little result; but he may be affected as he sees his sources of food, medicine, and morale being turned away from him. Another primary target is found in the government itself. All government officials must be convinced of their own value and purpose. Their humanitarian activities in the name of the government, such as civic actions, should actually serve to create and sustain a sense of national service, devotion to duty and country, and the sense of responsibility for others.

As an insurgency escalates and the subversive movement gains sufficient local or external support to initiate organized guerrilla warfare or other forms of violence against the established authority and its people, the psychological operations effort should shift its emphasis from environmental improvement to population and resources control. Long-range improvement plans must not be discarded, but the value of short-range, high-impact improvement programs will be more readily identified with the governmental interest in the people's problems than will projects taking years to complete. Civic action projects are well suited to this high psychological impact. Where the community has a need, this need should be met quickly by a cooperative effort between the local population and the military or paramilitary forces representing the government.

a. Population and Resources Control Programs. Control measures imposed in counterinsurgency curtail legitimate as well as subversive activities. The population must be forewarned of impending restrictions and the justification for them. They should be informed of benefits which will accrue from obedience and the hazards and penalties that will apply for violations of the regulations. Programs which often effectively isolate the guerrilla from his base of material and informational support include curfews; roadblocks and check points; control of food supplies; control of medical supplies; registration of all personnel, firearms, transportation, and fuels; establishment of "new life" hamlets for persons displaced by "clear and hold" operations; spot checks of cargoes in transit; and the isolation of key installations and areas. Each of these efforts will require a thorough study of the functional target groups and their key communicators. The target effectiveness and its susceptibility must be studied in light of the specific culture and the needs of that environment and the legitimate government. For this reason, vast and detailed amounts of sociological and anthropological information is required to develop a meaningful psychological operations campaign to change the attitudes and behavior of a specific group to favor governmental programs. The needs of the people must be matched and blended with the needs of the government. If people are convinced that it is in their best interest to support the government rather than the insurgents, then the controls and barriers may be removed. The people themselves will then willingly and actively assist the government in controlling the area.

b. Psychological Operations Programs Supporting Specific Population and Resources Control Programs. Specific programs which might be encountered during population and resources control operations are clear and hold operations and relocation operations. Clear and hold operations are concentrated in a specific, high priority area experiencing overt insurgency. Clear and hold operations are intended to create a secure physical and psychological environment and establish governmental control of the area. Psychological support of the clear and hold operations will assist in gaining the willing support of the population to obtain their participation in the governmental programs for counterinsurgency.

(1) *General considerations in clear and hold operations.* Since clear and hold operations expand outward from a secure base, programs should be conducted within the secure base to insure a high degree of support as well as to maintain unit and population morale. Psychological operations personnel must encourage host country agencies to stress proper conduct and behavior in dealings with the population. The military, paramilitary, and police often establish reputations of being oppressive, harsh, unsympathetic, and corrupt. Such reputations can be eliminated by proper conduct and through supporting propaganda campaigns which illuminate the positive actions and values of the forces. A few rash, undisciplined acts will jeopardize popular support and the entire operation. In an area to be cleared, initial psychological operations programs implemented should seek to make the population neutral. Clearly written and easily understood themes and directives should be used to encourage cooperation. Compensation should be made for damages if the operation occurs during the early phases of insurgency. The emphasis should be on equitable, rapid settlement of claims. At the same time, mili-

tary civic actions, such as medical assistance to injured civilians (consistent with the military situation and not detracting from the operational requirements of the mission) will reduce the hostility of the uprooted and injured people and will, with proper propaganda support, put the blame for the entire situation on the shoulders of the insurgents. The following are examples of propaganda announcements which might be appropriate: "Military operations and restrictions will be removed when support to the guerrillas ceases." "The bandits, supported by _____*, have destroyed the pleasant, good old days." "We must govern ourselves." "As long as the guerrilla is here, you will remain in the combat zone." If government forces are fresh and ready for action, psychological operations should encourage, even provoke, the guerrillas into standing and fighting. If they run, it will show their weakness and "cowardly" ways. In Asia, the insurgent's fear of fighting may be related to losing face, thus forcing him into a fight. Once engaged in battle, he may be fixed and destroyed.

(2) *Operational phases.* Once the area is cleared, the best psychological operations consist of informing the populace that the area is secure. To effect this, police or paramilitary forces should be recruited locally; and a sound training program should be initiated so that regular forces can be released for other missions. Psychological operations programs are designed to establish and maintain confidence among the newly created forces. Increased motivation of these forces can be achieved by such activities as parades and award ceremonies which recognizes desirable behavior such as bravery, community service, diplomacy, sacrifice, or honesty. Equitable treatment of popular forces, paramilitary forces, and regular military

or police units is essential to maintain esprit de corps and attain a sense of national unity. Host country dignitaries should be encouraged to visit and inspect the paramilitary forces. On such visits, the local leaders—political, military, religious, educational—should be recognized for their contributions and participation in community stability and development. This will contribute to a better understanding and communication between the national government and the local area and will commit the local leaders to the government.

(3) *Terminal phases.* Because tactical units are gradually withdrawn, consistent with the ability of paramilitary forces to assume responsibility for the area, psychological operations programs will come under more control of territorial or political subdivisions. Themes stressing the ultimate defeat of the guerrillas should be used. Items of local interest, even the establishment of a local newssheet, and local psychological operations teams are suitable for blending local with national goals and objectives. Such specific matters as governmental intentions for future, local, political organization and elections should be aired to give the population a sense of participation in their own affairs as well as the affairs of state.

(4) *General considerations in relocation operations.* Leaflets and loudspeaker messages should provide instructions about the impending move and should tell the people how to find transportation, if practical (promise of helicopter evacuation from guerrilla-dominated areas may increase the number of refugees). During the movement, special attention must be given to troop behavior because this may be the first impression of the recognized government. Instructions to the military units should include keeping families together, providing limited medical attention, assisting the refugees in a

165

warm and friendly manner, giving special attention to the aged and infirm. The initial impression received at the relocation center is important. It should be in advanced stages of construction, if possible, and include welcoming committees. Psychological operations should inform and entertain with subtle propaganda, explain ultimate plans for housing, medical assistance, and land distribution as appropriate, encourage covert exposure of guerrilla infiltrators and terrorists, and provide follow-up programs for continuity in the resettlement effort.

e. Illustrative Propaganda Themes. Leaflets, loudspeakers, radio, films, newspapers, and face-to-face persuasion can be used to disseminate symbolic propaganda designed to:

(1) Advertise the existence and accomplishments of the nation's programs.

(2) Persuade the local people, including guerrilla auxiliaries and underground elements, that their objectives can be obtained through specific, peaceful negotiation rather than through guerrilla warfare activities.

(3) Illustrate the futility and terrible cost of guerrilla warfare and its total effect upon the future of the nation.

(4) Show that the guerrilla movement has come under the control of a third power which is using the conflict to further its own ends in the area.

(5) Emphasize the fact that certain insurgent leaders are, in reality, bandits who seek the continuance of the war for their own personal gain.

(6) Bring the weight of international public opinion to bear upon third party nations actively supporting the guerrilla force in its attempts to overthrow the legitimate government.

(7) Explain the necessity for population control and guerrilla movement control operations.

(8) Expose the fallacies of the insurgent ideology.

d. Population and Resources Control Objectives. Under appropriate circumstances, these themes, and others dictated by the local environment, can be used in a counterinsurgent operation to create a favorable image of the legitimate government and to destroy the emotional attachment of the local people to the insurgent cause. The total defeat of the insurgent force occurs only when the real subversive causes of the insurgency have been uncovered and eliminated and when the minds of the population have been conditioned to support government programs and policies. Psychologically, the objective we seek is the cohesive support of all elements of the population for the legal government and its programs. To accomplish this, themes and programs should divide the major elements of the population from dissident elements seeking violent and terroristic change.

45. Psychological Operations Support of Counterguerrilla Operations

The military commander must be aware of not only the economic, sociological, and military issues, but also he must be aware of the psychological impact of each of these elements upon the population, his own troops, and the insurgents in each military operation conducted against the guerrillas. Having this awareness, it does not necessarily follow that a formalized psychological operations campaign would be included in every operation, but psychological values and problems would be considered. Ultimate success depends upon the leader's awareness of the perceptions of both the combatants and the non-combatants. Experience has shown that many commanders give too little emphasis to the psychological aspects of military operations. Too often, long-range political objectives are sacrificed for temporary tactical gains. Policy statements and guidance, properly written and enforced, would eliminate this problem.

a. In tactical situations, the psychological operations plan should include activities directed toward the insurgents, the civilian population in the immediate vicinity, and the troop command information program. For example, before or during an attack on a hamlet, civilians in the area should receive timely information concerning their role in the operation, possible benefits, or potential dangers. This information should be written in the local dialect to avoid any misunderstanding.

b. Maintaining the fighting spirit of the armed military and paramilitary forces is a top priority job. Higher pay, awards, promotions, and other prestige-related actions may be used to promote and sustain devotion and dedication to the nation in the face of what is obviously a dangerous job in an insurgency. Of utmost importance is the need for the government to present a picture of calm assurance of ultimate victory.

c. Divisive themes should be used towards the insurgents. There may be numerous well-intentioned insurgents. These people, whose sense of nationalism or frustration motivates them, should be separated from the subversive insurgents or Communist cadre. Proof of external support of the insurgents, personal intrigue, character traits contrary to the local culture, and divergent motivations are some examples of divisive themes which may be appropriate.

d. A nationally recognized amnesty program for the reintegration of insurgents who are captured or who surrender should be carefully planned and conducted. Amnesty ralliers should be carefully segregated from captured, hardcore, Communist cadre. The judicious use of propaganda throughout the retraining cycle would inform the amnesty ralliers of the governmental aid programs, and objectives and would contrast these against the subversive insurgent's methods, goals, and ambitions. Once the amnesty program is successfully implemented, every effort must be made to inform guerrillas of how and why they should rally under the provisions of the program. It is imperative that psychological operations supporting this program be centrally controlled, but the messages and themes should be primarily responsive to local needs and local insurgents. Aerial loudspeakers are ideally suited to this program and can get the message out to recently isolated guerrillas. Programs can be tailored to the motivations and susceptibilities of specific insurgent organizations which have just been beaten in battle, which are homesick, which recently have been filled with new recruits, or which have other known or suspected

vulnerabilities. By appealing to existing subconscious attitudes, the propagandist can direct these tendencies towards action and cause the individual to take the next opportunity to rally. It should be recognized that the situation must reinforce the tendency to defect before rallying will take place. To illustrate this, an insurgent may hate his leader whose harsh treatment of the platoon has made the recently drafted individual want to get out of such an irritating environment. A loudspeaker announcement telling how and where to rally would be prepared but it would not be used until it was safe to defect. Such an appeal would be used when others had begun known to have successfully rallied; when men have been separated from their control element by combat action; or when other similar conditions exist. The psychological operations program must convey the invitation to the insurgent when circumstances appear to reinforce his action tendencies.

e. Whatever the specific program to be implemented, the message must be designed and delivered so that it gains the attention of the insurgent. Common references and experiencs must be stressed to insure meaningful communications. The message must arouse the insurgent's needs and suggest ways of meeting these needs. The suggestion must be appropriate to the group and must relate to a situation affecting the insurgent at the time that the message is conveyed. All groups have established rules of behavior or roles that are played by the members based upon relationships or relative status. If group values are firmly held, it is highly unlikely that individuals would violate such group attitudes to achieve individual needs of a lower order of preference. A devout Jew will not eat ham. A normal American mother will not kill or harm her child. An Asian will not lose face. The psychological operations officer must have close relations with the intelligence community to determine these deeply held values and thus to optimize program acceptance in susceptible and effective target audiences. Similarly, an insurgent cadre will play his organizational role based upon his self-image and group expectations unless he is removed from that role by a change in situational factors: a demotion, a denunciation, etc.

"A direct surrender appeal, therefore would be unlikely to succeed since the cadreman would feel responsible for others and his self-image would cause him to enforce group standards of behavior.

46. Audience Consideration in an Insurgency

General. Since an insurgency is basically backed by numerous individuals who are opposed to all or part of the legally constituted governmental programs, ways and means must be devised to persuade a majority of these people that the government is not only serving their best interest but is the best qualified source of leadership for them. The vast majority of these people will be reached by mass media. Face-to-face persuasion and properly understood civic action programs are also extremely effective in appealing to the targets discussed below. Face-to-face communications have been found to be the most effective means of changing or forming attitudes because the man in the audience feels that he is then capable of judging credibility, sincerity, and the "real" interests and meaning of the speaker. Not only is face-to-face persuasion the most effective, but the propagandist may also take advantage of immediate feedback and modify the message to better suit the needs of the specific audience. Questions can be heard and answered. Wherever possible the propagandist must identify and appeal to "key communicators" and "opinion formers" within the selected target group(s) for they are the most influential in their field and scope. In spite of the need to appeal to functional groups, the following discussion is limited to the three principal groups within the insurgent nation: the government establishment, the civilian population, and the insurgents, for there are many generalizations which are of value.

Target. The Government Establishment. The military, paramilitary, civil service, and numerous other elements of the government establishment make an excellent target audience for several reasons. First, they should have a vested interest in seeing the government remain in control, ensuring their retention. Second, the chain-of-command or organizational structure is already established, making communications a natural and accepted thing. Third, these government representatives collectively and individually give the government its image. What they do or fail to do reflects the policy of the government either directly or indirectly, whether they recognize it or not.

(1) *Programs.* Specific programs should be initiated to promote respected behavior patterns; eliminate corruption, graft, and greed; promote sacrifice for the national good and service; promote a sense of responsibility to self, community, and government; encourage greater response to the needs and desires of the civil population; provide for local participation by the civilians in their own local government; eliminate the image of ruthlessness; inform the government establishment of governmental programs which are serving the developmental aims of the people; reward faithful governmental employees as a step in the long-range goals of eliminating subversive insurgency.

(2) *Actions.* Civic action programs, emphasizing self-help and cooperative efforts, are an example of the efforts which will perform two extremely important functions. Such programs will help convince the local citizens that the government is sincerely on their side. The governmental employees in their new role of benefactor, will begin assuming these responsibilities and become "the government with a conscience." This change from enforcer to helper is an overt commitment which will irrevocably change the personality and attitude of individuals and groups if properly conducted and supervised. Those involved will be participants in the development of their country, hopefully committed to the service of the people and the government.

(3) *Initiative.* Seizing the economic, political, social, and military initiative is important in achieving a complete vic-

tory over the subversive insurgents. When on the defensive, only temporary and short-range victories can be achieved. The majority of countries beset with insurgency are predominantly agrarian, therefore, the governments which remain within the urban areas, either physically or psychologically, will remain defensive and will lose. The government should adopt themes which might be used by the insurgents, depriving them of the psychological advantage. Insurgents must be kept on the defensive while the government remains on the attack and retains the initiative.

(4) *Advantages.* The image of a people's government, regardless of its exact form, will create a cooperative attitude within the population. Rapport will permit the government access to information and support and will accelerate the elimination of the insurgency.

c. Target. The Civilian Population. In addition to the psychological objectives mentioned under developing national unity, there are other important factors to consider when addressing the civilian population; but the need to stress ultimate victory is paramount. The people will remain either apathetic or hostile if there is doubt about the government's ability to win and retain control; because Communists, when taking over an area, normally liquidate, through "popular trials," those who have supported the government. Supporters of the former, recognized, legal government who are not liquidated are usually sent to schools where their self-guilt is built up and they develop symptoms of withdrawal as the Communist thought-reform web of vertical and horizontal controls slowly enmeshes and strangles them in the name of the state. One can understand, in this light, the reluctance to support the legal government until it is relatively clear that the government shall win.

(1) *Programs.* Informational programs and services are required at several levels. At the national level, common governmental aspirations, goals, and programs should be publicized. These national programs should be benevolent and beneficial. They should be couched in terms that permit the local political, economic, and social leaders to interpret and adopt them to meet local needs. At the local level, the population should be able to see readily an image of good government, working with and for the people. These programs aimed at the civilian population must be coordinated at a national level so that they will not be applied in a counterproductive to military and military psychological operations. An image of good government and unity of effort to achieve the national programs to the maximum, positive information programs should be designed to motivate the people to support the government against a politically motivated, subversive insurgent threat which is externally controlled and supported. National unity programs which reinforce governmental programs should be implemented and popular support of such programs should be encouraged. National unity objectives must be stressed to pre-school, primary school, secondary school, university students, and all other youth activity functional groups in order to foster the development of national pride and a sense of national responsibility. All other organizations throughout the country should be encouraged to demonstrate their support on a voluntary basis: and rewards and considerations can be developed to reinforce desirable, cooperative behavior. Although outward manifestation of governmental support does not always mean active physical and moral support, such a show will tend to undermine the insurgent's morale and create an illusion of isolation. The many who are uncommitted will also get the impression that the population offers mas-

sive, unanimous support of the government.

(2) *Advantages.* Since the popular support of the insurgents is essential to the victory or even the continued existence of a significant subversive insurgency, the population is one of the major psychological targets of the insurgents. It must also be a key target of the legitimate government's psychological operations program. The government has access to the target audience during the incipient stages of insurgency and in the phases of insurgency before complete loss of control within an area. The audience can be readily studied and reached until the threat becomes so severe that the population is afraid to support the government. The people who are frustrated within the developing nation will respond favorably to the first propagandist who offers a reasonable solution to their frustrations. The threatened government has to recognize the problems and point the people towards the governmental solutions of these problems, thereby forcing the insurgent to react to the government's effort instead of taking the initiative. The insurgent must be compelled to assume the defensive. The insurgents must not be permitted to sow their seeds in an environment of unmitigated frustrations and anxieties. The government must recognize the political nature of the subversive threat and must plan and execute an effective counter program. The burden is upon the government and its advisors to recognize the problem and to correct it. Society, with its inertia and desire to remain in a reasonably stable condition, with reasonable rules of law, and with known interrelationships, is more receptive to developmental propaganda than to revolutionary promises and blandishments. Adverse conditions must be sought and corrected early in order to benefit the government. Once the issues

have been aired by both sides, the rule of law is in dispute, and active guerrilla and terrorist activities are being conducted, the psychological operations initiative may still be regained by properly planning a campaign supporting the internal defense plans.

d. Target. The Insurgent. Since a determined insurgency gathers momentum in direct proportion to the attractiveness of the ideology upon which the movement is based, the highly motivated insurgent may not be vulnerable to propaganda. Below them, however, within both the vertical political organization and the horizontal functional group organizations, there are a number of vulnerable individuals and groups. These susceptible individuals and groups can be propagandized effectively to benefit the government and to achieve national objectives.

(1) *Programs.* Programs which may be successful against insurgents would include the following themes: divisive themes, working on differences between cadre, recruits, supporters, and the local population; anti-morale themes such as defeats, lack of support, isolation, homesickness, hardships, shortages, etc., illegal and terroristic actions (being careful not to create an image which will cause the civilians to cower before the insurgent) may be used to focus civilian hostility against the insurgent; amnesty themes may be used to exploit any tendency towards action which may develop as a result of attitude changes; and rewards may be offered for select insurgent leaders for various crimes. Leniency should be reflected by the government and all of its agencies rather than the pursuit of dogmatic standards of innocence versus guilt. All such programs should recognize the differences in status and origin of the insurgents. Specific, very localized messages, resulting from current, accurate intelligence, will yield maximum return on the propaganda aimed towards the insurgents and their local supporters.

(2) *Actions.* All media may be used against insurgents; however, since they are normally closely controlled and guarded against host government propaganda, they are often inaccessible to television, movies, radio, and printed media. Nevertheless, many ingenious methods may be devised to overcome these handicaps and increase communication with the insurgents. Safe conduct and amnesty leaflets have been found effective when readily available and easily secreted by the insurgent. Every effort should be made to take advantage of any fears which the insurgents develop or hold with respect to the government forces, their weapons or any assistance the host country might be getting. Additional programs are discussed in chapter 4, FM 33-1.

Section III. SUBVERSIVE PROPAGANDA OBJECTIVES AND ORGANIZATION

47. General

In an insurgency the enemy is difficult to identify, since he cannot be readily engaged in combat nor does he display consistencies and patterns. Consistencies are found, however, in externally controlled or sponsored subversive insurgencies. These consistencies, once recognized, enable the propagandist to better combat the threat. The insurgency will have certain recognizable objectives, methods, and organizations which make its appeals and false blandishments readily accepted and difficult to eliminate.

48. Subversive Insurgent Psychological Objectives

a. One psychological objective of the insurgent is to convince the local populace that local goals and aspirations are identical to those of the insurgent. In its formative stages, an insurgency is weak and needs to identify itself with the goals and aspirations of the local population. Typical themes which have enabled insurgencies to achieve the image of popular heroes are anti-colonialism, nationalism, and land reform. By aligning themselves with popular aspirations, the insurgents gain a number of positive reactions from attitudes which are formed about their activities while they are ostensibly serving the best interests of the people. Local insurgent leaders normally will not admit external controls and relations but will hold up their liberation mission for the ultimate freedom and independence of the people. By proving external sponsorship, the image of "national hero" can often be destroyed.

b. A second insurgent objective is to convince significant portions of the population that their interests are not best served by the government due to recognized, psychological weaknesses. Developing nations whose international boundaries have been arbitrarily established often have engulfed powerful groups (tribes, clans, extended families, and religious sects) which have been controlled and separated by an alien party such as a colonial power. Once independence has been achieved and the former arbiter is removed from the scene, the power balance normally shifts rapidly. Groups which had been held in check become free to express their discontent with the new power structure. Subversive insurgents look for these psychological weaknesses and vulnerabilities to exploit. Timely use of forces thus created can facilitate the establishment of a new power balance and lead to ultimate seizure of power by the insurgents. Social, economic, political, ethnic, and religious minorities are typical groups which should be studied to determine the nature and extent of their frustrations and the degree of danger they represent to the legal government. There are also majority groups which must be studied in this same light, including peasants in an agricultural economy, workers in industrialized areas, and youths and women in a transitional society. These faceless masses can be organized and rallied to causes and ideologies which claim to give them immediate,

34

over-simplified answers or releases from their frustrations.

c. A third objective of the insurgent is to convince the country that the government and its leadership is unworthy of leading the people. The presence of graft, greed, corruption, nepotism, scandal, and infinite varieties of other faults make it very difficult, if not impossible, to hide from the insurgent propagandist's probes. The insurgent propagandist will question people and determine those areas where there are common complaints along economic, moral, or political grounds. He will then provide governmental scapegoats on which the people can vent their feelings. Even such problems as droughts, floods, and other natural calamities which create anxieties and frustrations will be used by the insurgents to "reveal" the government's incompetence.

d. Another psychological objective of the insurgent is to destroy national morale and confidence in the government. Once the insurgent cadre are trained and properly organized, they begin gnawing away at the governmental structure in outlying rural or mountainous areas. These areas are so remote that the incidents and terroristic activities destroy the fabric of law and order under the legal government (if it existed before), and the government can do little to provide necessary safety without an undue expenditure of its scarce power resources. Both the local inhabitants and the subversive insurgents recognize the government's helplessness once insurgent forces have been organized and established in these remote areas. It becomes then extremely difficult for the government to reestablish confidence in the legally constituted government, primarily because of sanctions and retribution which the insurgents exact from the local population the instant the government forces depart. Signs of cooperation with the government are sure to cause the individual to be punished after a self-criticism session. Through covert actions the guerrillas begin expanding from clandestine bases using selective terror tactics to create an environment of fear, while showing that the government cannot protect the people or properly administer the area. By illustrating the ineptitude of the government

and at the same time placing their own shadow government in every hamlet and village, they begin taking over the administrative functions of government. Ultimately, the government is left in its barracks and compounds and the insurgents and people are left to the rest of the country. National morale or a sense of unity as a nation-state is virtually nonexistent at the time of independence, and it is a simple matter for the insurgents to continuously force the government to show its brutal, harsh, and arbitrary nature through its counterinsurgent tactics. The insurgent encourages the government to create an image of ruthlesness by forcing it to carry out indiscriminate artillery and aircraft bombing of hamlets where insurgents have been supported or by any of the many other uses of force to destroy the insurgents and their bases.

e. Another psychological objective of the insurgent is to convince the world and the local population that the motives of nations assisting the threatened government are false. Through national and international media, the insurgent will attempt to malign the motives of all assistance to the local government. Economic exploitation, neo-colonialism, genocide, and capitalism seeking raw materials and markets are some of the numerous themes used to elicit sympathy and support.

f. Another objective of the insurgent is to convince the people that the insurgents will win the political struggle. Both the insurgent and the government will have this program in common. Popular support will be afforded to the side which is most likely to win. If the contest is in doubt, the people may be apathetic with willing, open support being difficult to gain for either side. Although the side with the greatest organizational and leadership capability will have a decided advantage. The insurgents have both vertical and horizontal organizations which provide administrative control. Their horizontal control organizations provide not only for participation, but for propaganda as well. Threatened governments, as currently constituted, seldom have organizations which could generate a voluntary sense of belonging to the nation, nor do they recognize the need for the populace to be able to express itself. The government is compelled to use the older organizations, denying their use to the insurgent. This gives the insurgent a big opening with the restless youth, women, and farmers who cannot express themselves under the legal regime. Thus, many governments use traditional devices which keep feelings of frustration alive among the population, and reduce or slow down the rate at which modernization and development can be instituted. In addition to this organizational advantage, the insurgent is also able to leap upon the theories which have been propounded by Marx, Lenin, and Mao Tse-tung to illustrate the inevitability of the downfall of capitalism and the victory of socialism, communism, peoples democracies, or anything else they may desire to prove through dialectic interpretation of these revolutionary leaders. Selectively exploiting surprise, ambushes, and traps, the insurgent leaders can tell their forces of great victories; and at the same time, since they control their media closely, they can minimize the effect of defeats. They emphasize their military, economic, social, and political accomplishments and either avoid or "interpret" negative issues.

g. Insurgent leaders also attempt to convince every guerrilla, supporter, and sympathizer that he or she should be a propagandist. Schools, propagandist speeches, cultural shows, books, and radio programs are used to give the people in insurgent controlled areas a controlled understanding of the situation. However, the real energy and force for the insurgency comes from the cadre training programs where a fanatic zeal is developed. The cadre are highly motivated through a series of traumatic training sessions. Once trained, these cadre go out to establish and organize their home-town regions. Through the selective use of terror and the threat of violence, the nonbeliever, isolated from all group supports which would oppose the insurgent cause, is forced into compliance with insurgent aims and objectives. Even nonbelievers comply with instructions to strike, tarry, and assist through unspoken or implied threats. Through proper control of media, messages, and situational environment, numerous willing supporters can be and are elicited. These misguided people are not easily reconverted to the government side, but must be differentiated from the insurgent cadre.

49. Subversive Insurgent Propaganda Organization

a. Targets. Subversive insurgents avoid disseminating propaganda in a vacuum. They act on the premise that the most effective propaganda is aimed at an audience which is already partly committed to their cause. The emergence of an audience so psychologically captured depends upon the prior creation of an elaborate system of controls. This is not to infer that the government establishment and the general population at large does not receive subversive propaganda, but rather that the greatest effort is expended against those over whom the insurgents have control (whether total or just during the hours of darkness).

b. Controls. The system of controls established is of both a physical and a psychological nature. The controls allow for the subtle blending of both positive appeals (such as promises of an actual redistribution of land in a village) and negative sanctions for nonconformity. The sanctions run the gamut of emotional appeals from isolation and rejection from certain group activities to self-criticism, group accusation, and group criticism; to 6-week visits to remote training camps, to death. Unrepentant landlords and usurers are often given the harshest sentences to prove the sincerity of the insurgent government in dealing harshly with those who do not hold the best interest of the people foremost. The local population is often required to sit in judgment in such cases. When the verdict of guilty is announced, the people are asked if the individual should be granted leniency, thereby showing the lenient, benevolent nature of this "people's government." Such controls on individuals are maintained and intensified in a consistent fashion by the political organization of the target area. Insurgent leaders insist on strict organizational discipline among their cadre. Once this discipline is established, they demand discipline among the target group.

AGO 5745A

This vertical organization is one key to effective control and dissemination of propaganda. It characteristically takes months or even years to establish the shadow political organization. At the same time, certain horizontal organizations are formed which act as propaganda transmission belts. Both of these two basic organizations are responsive to a unified, central, political command at any given level of administration (village, district, regional, etc.).

c. *Vertical Organization.* The primary function of the vertical-political organization is to administer both the command system and the training of new administrative cadres. In an insurgent-controlled, "liberated" area, the organizational structure at the village level would be headed by the village party secretary, assisted by a deputy secretary. Responsible to them would be various subsections or committees (economic and finance, security, education, culture, etc.). Cadre would fill these political posts. They would listen to radio broadcasts from Hanoi, Peking, or other Communist sources and adapt the issues discussed by these sources directly to the local issues. One week the international stress may be on anti-Americanism; another it may be anti-colonialism. In this way, the local insurgent jumps on the band-wagon and benefits from news around the world as well as from locally generated illustrations and propaganda.

d. *Horizontal Organizations.* The horizontal organizations are designed to satisfy the human need to participate. These mass organizations are organized and controlled by the subversive insurgent cadre. Occasionally a recognized local leader will become titular head of these front organizations to provide an image of popular support and participation. The mass associations are designed to encompass everyone in the community and are given names which imply broad participation such as: *Liberation Women, Liberation Youth, Liberation Farmers,* and *Liberation Workers.* In a controlled area, initially, everyone must belong to at least one such organization; the individual is then given certain tasks and responsibilities which he must accomplish in the name of the "people's" organization. If he shirks these tasks, he must confess or have

people single him out as a malingerer. The cadres encourages each individual to extend his affiliations with other "liberation" groups, thereby increasing his responsibilities to the point of total absorpton of his time in the cause of insurgency, while the cause is never committed to the individual. The individual is closely supervised and criticized to the point that he develops a sense of pseudo-paranoia. He feels that everyone is watching his every move and that he is slowly, but surely, being isolated and insulated from the functional groups to which he formerly belonged. While this process is going on, the organization continuously makes him commit himself to the "people's" cause and persuades him to participate in communal activities. Gradually, these organizations take over all social, political, economic, cultural, and military controls. The isolation and fear generated in the individual makes it all but impossible to collectively fight the system.

e. *Purpose of the Organization.* The individual is encouraged to participate, always in an atmosphere controlled by the skilled agitation and propaganda cadres. Such participation is the real meaning of "people's democracy" in a "liberated area." Once the vertical and horizontal organizations have been carefully established, a potent and controlled arena for incessant subversive propaganda exists. The vertical organization replaces the legally constituted government. The horizontal organizations give the necessary facade of democracy, for these mass propaganda organizations permit the people "to express and discuss their problems," even solve their problems, so long as there is no conflict with the insurgent, vertical organizations and the party cadre. Therefore, these closely knit, intertwined control organizations must be unravelled and disentangled before psychological operations personnel can reach effective and susceptible target audiences within "liberated areas." The best solution is to foresee the political nature of the problem and forewarn the legal government and as many of the people as possible so that the people will know what the real nature of the choice is. Whether the "liberated areas" are lost by political naivete or conquered by default, the patterns and consistencies are available for study.

Phung Hoang (Phoenix) Comic Book (Valentine, Addendum 1)

Caption 4. Following is the news: "This morning at nine A.M., a Lambretta was blown up by a Communist mine five kilometers outside Phung Hiep village. Two children were killed, three women wounded. The Communists continue to terrorize people!'"

Caption 5. "Hello, sister Tu!" "Why are you so late?" "Hello, brother and sister. I am sorry I am late. I left early this morning, but we had to stop at the bridge because it was destroyed by a Communist bomb. We had to wait for the bridge to be repaired by a military engineering unit."

Caption 6. "Mr. Ba, you are asked to pay farm tax to the Liberation Front!"

176

Caption 7. "This year the crop is poor, but the Communists still collect taxes. It is a miserable situation. I have heard there is much security in Phung Phu village. There taxes are not collected by the Communists any more thanks to the Phoenix operation. I wonder why such an operation has not come to our village?"

"Perhaps because nobody provides them with information! This afternoon the Phoenix operation agents posted a notice at the intersection. I will go and see it tomorrow."

Caption 8. "What is new, my friends?"

"There are two dangerous Communist cadres hiding in our village."

Caption 9. Here are the two Communist cadres sought by the Phoenix Operation. The wanted poster says: "Dear compatriots, If you know the hiding place of the two above-named Communist cadres, please notify the national police or the armed forces. You will be rewarded, and your name will be kept secret."

Caption 10. The radio broadcast says, "Compatriots, please help your government by providing information indicating the hiding place of two Communists, Ba Luong and Hai Gon. You will be rewarded, and your name will be kept secret."

"Did you hear that on the radio?"

"I knew it already. It is exactly the same as it has been posted on the wall at the intersection of the village."

Caption 11. "See, there are so many leaflets!"

Caption 12. "Honey, what do they say in those leaflets?"

"They are the same as those wall posters, as well as the announcements on the radio yesterday. The two Communists Ba Luong and Hai Gon are presently hiding in our village in order to collect taxes. I am determined to report to the Phoenix Operation Committee because I know their hiding place."

Caption 13. "Where are you going so early?"

"I am going to the district headquarters to report about what happened last night."

Caption 14. "Dear Sir, the two Communists you want are hiding in my village. They are hiding in the house number 80/2 by my village boundaries. They only go out at night. If you succeed in arresting them, please keep my name secret!"

"Thank you, Mr. Ba, your name will be kept secret." (The Phoenix Operation provides security and prosperity to the people.)

Caption 15. "Why are so many soldiers entering our village?"

"Perhaps they are conducting a military operation against the Communists in hiding."

Caption 16. "The two Communists are very dangerous. We can only have peace and security when they are captured."

Caption 17. "Ladies, do you know that the two Communists are captured? From now on our village will be secure. There will be no more assassinations or tax collectors. The Phoenix operation is very effective!"

Caption 18. "Mr. Ba, since the two Communists are captured, our village is at peace. Too bad they are in jail! If they returned to our side beforehand, it could have been better for them!"

"They are obstinate indeed. Had they returned like Mr. Thanh from Long Dien village, they certainly would have enjoyed the government's clemency. Mr. Thanh is now reunited with his family."

Caption 19. "Mr. Ba, you have some mail."

"I wonder who sends you this mail?"

"Wait and see!"

Caption 20. "What does the letter say?"

"Dear Mr. Ba, Since you have helped the government by providing information and undermining the local structures of the Communists, you will be rewarded accordingly. You are invited to attend the coming meeting of the Phoenix Operation Committee to receive your award. Sincerely yours."

Caption 21. Poster says: "Mr. Nguyen Van Thanh, former guerrilla at Long Dien village, Gia Rai District, Bac Lieu Province, has returned to the national side. He therefore is allowed to be reunited with his family."

APPENDIX C

Lecture Transcript, Edward Lansdale, Military Psychological Operations: Part One

Lecture, Armed Forces Staff College
Norfolk, Virginia, 7 January 1960
By: Colonel Edward G. Lansdale, USAF
     (Deputy Assistant to the Secretary of
     Defense, Special Operations)

MILITARY PSYCHOLOGICAL OPERATIONS

I.

In our brief time together today, I plan to introduce you to the oldest weapon known to man outside of bare hands -- psychological warfare. As bright and bushy-tailed staff officers, you will need to know what psychological warfare is, how it fits into the scheme of military affairs today, and how to use it most wisely.

II.

First of all, then, what is psychological warfare? It is an action, usually propaganda, which you take to influence the will of other people, usually the enemy, to support the gaining of your military objective in war.

Some examples will illustrate this definition: Joshua's use of noise at Jericho -- and modern usage, such as bugle-blowing by the Chinese Communists in Korea. Tamerlane's piling up the bones of the slain into a huge pyramid at one conquered city to show to envoys from other cities and frightening them into surrender -- and the blackmail of nations by Hitler with his newsreel movies of Stuka-Panzer teams in action. The tatooing of the arms of his soldiers by Tran Hung Dao to stiffen their will to defeat Kublai Khan -- and such modern concepts as, "make the world safe for Democracy" or "the Four Freedoms."

Now, hardly a day goes by without a military officer suddenly discovering "psychological warfare" -- most often by discovering some clever attack by the Communists -- and then becoming enthusiastic over this "wonder weapon", believing that if we adopted it strongly, we would have little need of anything else. Also, hardly a day goes by without some military officer dismissing psychological warfare as a non-military item invented on Madison Avenue and belonging in the category of, say, PX officers or the school for cooks and bakers. As staff officers, you must be wary and not fall into either trap.

Think of psychological warfare as a weapon . . . not as propaganda posters, or as surrender leaflets, or as radio programs beamed at foreigners . . . but as a weapon, like artillery, or torpedoes, or guided missiles. Our military staffs have learned to integrate these other weapons into our operational plans. So it is, also, with psychological warfare. The proper use of this weapon should be included in every combat plan you make -- as an important, supporting weapon that will help achieve military victory.

III.

In what has been said so far, note that psychological warfare has been identified with war and with actual combat. In the U.S. Armed Forces, this is how we associate psychological warfare.

What then about today, when we are not in combat -- but when the military has so significant a role in implementing national policy? Certainly, there is need for psychological support of today's military activities.

Well, we do have psychological operations today. We have built a familiar American structure to carry them out -- complex organizations, civilian groups to carry the main burden in peace-time, and different names so that the work can be fractionalized to suit the jurisdictional gremlins. However, the important thing for you to remember is this: some place in the combined or unified staff where you will serve some day, you will find a staff group charged with planning today's psychological operations and the future's possible psychological warfare. Let's see where this staff section fits into today's U.S. structure.

As do the Soviets and the Chinese Communists, as do our British friends, as our French friends are starting to do -- so too do we have a marriage of the civil-political and the military for top direction of psychological operations. This is logical, because we must have a political basis for our actions if our psychological operations are to be successful. National objectives dictate psychological objectives.

National policy, and thus the policy for psychological operations, comes from topside -- the President, as our political leader and as our Commander-in-Chief, aided by the National Security Council. In wartime, for theaters of war, the direction would come simply down the chain-of-command. In today's peacetime, direction for foreign operations comes through the State Department to Defense, either directly or by its chairing and steering the OCB and the OCB committees. It is often misunderstood, but the decisive voice today in our national foreign operations is that of the State Department, not that of Defense, the JCS, the Services or Commands. Under State Department guidance, the U.S. Information Agency is charged with carrying out psychological operations abroad. In wartime, most of USIA's people and resources abroad would come under military direction.

In Defense, top guidance comes from the Secretary of Defense -- meaning Secretary Gates who is personally interested, Deputy Secretary Douglas who has decisive responsibilities, and their immediate staff. On

-5-

this immediate staff, the Assistant to the Secretary for Special Operations has the main burden for this task.

In the Joint Staff, the planning and staff work of psychological operations is carried out by the Joint Subsidiary Activities Division of J-5. Each of the Armed Services has a staff section for psychological warfare, as part of operations. In the Military Commands, the J-3 or the G-3 has a staff section for psychological warfare.

Remember these military psychological planners when you start working on operational plans. Always include a section in your planning for psychological support. We have paid a costly price since 1945 for neglecting the psychological part of our operations until recently and let the Communists get way ahead of us. We cannot afford any more neglect.

IV.

Now, let's have a brief time with some of today's psychological operations.

Although, as staff officers, you will be concerned mostly with strategic planning, it will be more useful to you today if I deal with tactical operations. This should help give you a more basic understanding of the weapon. It's not much good to plan the strategic use of a weapon, if you don't know what it can do.

Several weeks ago, Leon Delbecque visited Washington and we had a chance to talk with each other. He is the French Deputy who sparked the formation of the Fifth Bureau in the French Army and the operations of its Revolutionary Warfare in Algeria. We agreed that there were many fine technicians in Psychological Warfare today, that many of the staff officers in both Armed Forces were long on book theory but short on practical application, and that the best psychological operator is born rather than trained to the job.

M. Delbecque said that he picked his best operators in Algeria by looking over personal history statements, and selecting officers and men who had had to work with their hands for a living at one time in their civilian life. It gave them an instinctive empathy for the people whom they had to influence.

This reminded me of a similar problem in the Tonkin Delta of Indo-China in 1953. General Cogny was strengthening his psychological warfare organization then and invited my comment. I recommended that he fill the organization with officers and men with good combat records, those who knew the enemy best through fighting him and who were rotating out of the

-3-

184

line -- and with, I hoped, a ribald sense of humor. Humor -- bawdy humor, slapstick, the practical joke, and Olympian humor -- all can add the final touch of practical effectiveness to a psychological operation.

Not long ago, in England, the Communists inspired an anti-American campaign. Painted letters saying "Go Home Yank" started appearing on walls. A bright individual visited these signs and painted in the addition, "via TWA." The British were highly amused and the campaign stopped.

The Agit-Prop folks of the Viet Cong Communist Party in North Vietnam have a macabre sense of humor. About this time last year, they sent an agent in to poison the food at the prison camp of Phu Loi in South Vietnam. At the deadline time they had given the agent for his operation, before he had a chance to report, Radio Hanoi went on the air with simulated outrage against the Americans in MAAG-Vietnam for poisoning a thousand prisoners at Phu Loi. Later, it was changed to ten thousand. It didn't matter that no American had visited the prison at Phu Loi. It didn't matter that their agent had cold-feet at the last moment and failed to carry out his assignment. Nobody was poisoned at Phu Loi. Yet, it was a joke with a pay-off. The workers of North Vietnam contributed days of free labor, the school students collected funds -- for the highly-publicized "victims" -- funds the Party could use. The Americans in MAAG and the Free Vietnamese have hardly found this funny. But then, the victims of bad jokes seldom do. Perhaps, some day, the people in North Vietnam will also catch on. This is part of mankind's hope today.

In 1950, I found myself serving as an adviser to the Philippine Armed Forces on various aspects, including psychological warfare, of their campaign against Communist Huk guerrillas. This was in the lull after World War II. We had no Psywar organizations or training in our Services, so as a substitute I talked to everyone I could find who had had psywar experience in World War II. I will pass along to you the most useful lesson I learned from them -- a combat concept which they called "The Eye of God." It has many variations. Maybe, some day, you will remember this in an hour of need and it will help you.

The "Eye of God" technique, properly used, makes the target soldier feel that he is the helpless victim of an all-seeing and all-powerful enemy. This was the basic idea behind the broadcasts of Berlin Sally and Toyko Rose, when they would specify units by name and tell them the contents of their secret orders. This was the basic idea, also, of the examples given me. One was the siege of Caen in the Normandy Invasion, where the French Maquis kept the British well informed of the exact whereabouts of key German officers. The psywar team, through loud-speakers, would warn a German general by name that if his forces didn't surrender immediately, he would die. A little later, as he sat in his headquarters office, an artillery shell would zero in and get him. This was team-work between Maquis intelligence, the psywarriors, and the artillery. It paid off in the surrender of Caen.

This team-work was later adapted by Americans to an air-armor team. Loud-speakers were mounted on tanks. The tanks were in communication with a liaison aircraft overhead. German infantry, dug-in in hidden positions which could be seen from the air, would be surprised when a tank would appear and speak to them: "You twenty soldiers on the hill -- Yes, you sergeant crawling over to the left -- all you soldiers -- You stay there and we will kill you." This made the war personal. This made the threat personal. Faced with talking armor, most troops thus singled out would run or surrender.

In the Philippines, in 1950 and 1951, we used many variations. In one -- to encourage the growing intelligence nets on our side, who often were dealt with savagely by the Huks, and to throw fear into the Huks and their sympathizers that they were being watched continuously -- troops would sneak into a barrio at night and paint big, staring eyes on the sides of houses. This increased tensions for the already tense Huk guerrilla enemy. Constant tension brought fatigue. A fatigued soldier makes mistakes, particularly when he faces constant, aggressive patrol action against him.

A more direct application of the technique was used against small, hit-and-run Huk squadrons. Their presence in an area would be reported by the Army intelligence net. When troops would move against them, enemy intelligence nets would warn the Huk squadrons - and they would take off fast before contact could be made. The problem was how to make contact and inflict casualties on a wary, hit-and-run enemy.

The Philippine Army put the only available P.A. systems -- they were Navy loud-hailers intended for beach masters, with hand-carried electric megaphones -- into liaison aircraft, L-5's. When one of the hit-and-run Huk squadrons was reported, the psywar and intelligence officers of the battalion in the area would go over all the Order of Battle information they had on the Huk squadron. Armed with this information and his loud-hailer, the battalion psywar officer would be flown by the liaison aircraft to the spot where the Huk squadron was hiding.

Circling over them, the psywar officer would talk to the hidden Huks by name with his amplified voice: "You hiding down there . . . we see you. Yes, I mean you in Squadron 17. I mean you, Commander Sol. I mean you, Juan Santos. And you, Bulacan Boy. And you, Pepe. We are coming to kill you. We know all about you. Stay there. We will kill you. And now, I must go while our troops are coming. To our secret friend in your ranks, I say thank you -- run and hide so you won't be killed. Sorry, I can't call

-5-

you by name -- but thank you and good-bye."

Of course, there was no "friend in the ranks." The Order of Battle information had come from many sources, carefully put together over the weeks. But, the broadcast from the air usually stampeded the Huk squadron. They would leave their hiding place on the run. And then suspicion would start working. Who was this "friend in the ranks?" Which one of the comrades was a secret enemy spy? One or more of the comrades looked suspicious. A quick kangaroo court would be held -- the suspected judged guilty and executed. Thus, some information adroitly used, would bring about the same number of casualties as could a company of troops in a running fight.

V.

Now, it is time to close this little talk. I hope it has awakned your interest in military psychological operations. If it has, there are many books on the subject from which you can learn more. One is readily available to you and is well worth reading. It is the Army Field Manual on "Psychological Warfare Operations", FM 33-5, and contains many ideas and descriptions of techniques.

But, if you don't have time to read, then please remember something from the talk this morning. You and every other military man in the Free World is the target of some of the most skilled psychological attack the world has ever seen. If the Communists deem this attack worth so very much of their resources -- in talented manpower and huge budgets -- then don't be ignorant of this powerful weapon when you plan the use of resources on our side. Be alert to the fact that it exists. Include it in the plans you work on as staff officers. On the staff with you will be a section devoted to psychological warfare. Let them in on your planning, to come up with specific plans for the psychological support of the operation. In this way, you can help us use a fine weapon which we have overlooked too often -- a weapon we need today to help us achieve our national objectives.

Thank you.

APPENDIX D

Lecture Transcript, Edward Lansdale, Military Psychological Operations: Part Two

Lecture - Armed Forces Staff College, Norfolk, Virginia
9 March 1960
By: Colonel Edward G. Lansdale
     Office of the Secretary of Defense

MILITARY PSYCHOLOGICAL OPERATIONS: PART TWO

I.

I have been told that each of you has been given a copy of the talk I gave to the last class in January. The talk was really an introduction to the subject of "military psychological operations", sketching in some definitions, some history, how we are organized to operate, and describing one successful operating technique for combat.

Questions by the class after the last talk led me to conclude that perhaps the most helpful thing I could do in our brief time together today would be to discuss "how to operate", rather than the organizational side of the operations. So, I will talk to you as potential operators. Then, as bright and bushy-tailed staff officers in the future, you might remember what a psychological operation actually is--and be better able to fit it in with your staff planning.

Today, I will sketch in the basic operational rules. Then, I will give you some case histories of operations against the Communists. The one should help you remember the other.

II.

Psychological warfare is probably man's oldest weapon, aside from bare hands. In using it in today's dirty, little, secretive wars, or in the future, the important thing to remember is that it is a weapon--and that a weapon has its own unique use and its own effect.

I have observed a bad trend in too many of our psychological operations today. We have advanced technically in making this weapon more effective and have attracted some very bright technicians to work with this psychological weapon. In turn, they become bemused with the technical side and seem to forget that what they have is a weapon--a weapon that is meant to cause desired results. They remind me of artillerymen toiling for long hours to perfect the firing of salutes. We can applaud their precision in the firing of blank ammunition, but they and we must not forget that artillery has a more practical task in war.

1

So, let's get down to the fundamentals of using the psychological weapon. As fundamentals, these are simple things. Being simple, they are overlooked at times when operators strive to be sophisticated, "big picture" artists. When firing for effect, we cannot afford such fancies. We must insist upon following the basic rules.

The rules are these:

First, be sure of your command's politico-military _objective_ and stick with it in your operations.

Second, know exactly what you want to cause people to _do_ as a result of each of your operations.

Third, put across your activating idea in a way that these people will _understand_.

III.

Now, for the first rule. Our ultimate objective is always a political one--whether the immediate objective is that of destroying an enemy's armed force as _his_ instrument for reaching his political objective, or something else. Know what your command's real goal is, know it thoroughly--and don't waste your energy, skill, and material resources in going elsewhere.

You need a clear appreciation of the moment of history in which you live, how our policy believes it must be guided to history's next moment for the good of the country, and just what part your command plays in this. It is known that the Communist enemy, right down through his command to small units, has _his_ clear idea of this. To fight him successfully, you must have yours.

IV.

Now, the second rule.

The psychological weapon is used to make people _do_ something. So, you have to think out very clearly just what it is, exactly, that you want to cause people to do. This step is all-important. Make your objective realistic, "bite-size", something you can bring about definitely. Do you want the enemy to hesitate before squeezing a trigger, to disobey orders of his commander, to move to an area of your choice, to desert, to do what--exactly? The more clearly you know what you want him to do, the more effective will be your use of this weapon. Be fuzzy about this, and your results will be fuzzy--no matter how beautifully you print leaflets, no matter how skillfully you use electronic equipment.

V.

So, in waging psychological warfare, you must be sure of your objective since you are on the scene with a weapon which can be very powerful, you must know exactly what result you want, and then you must obey the third rule.

The third rule is to put across your idea in an understandable way to the people you want to have react. What they will react to is not necessarily what you react to. There is no sense in printing leaflets for people who cannot read, in using precocious ideas which might be diverting at a cocktail party but which shrink to nothing under primal needs, in assaying the terroristic superstitions of jungle or rice paddy in terms of a Pennsylvania farmyard, regardless of how close these seem to you as a foreigner. Get your activating idea across in terms and in a way that the receivers will understand, accept, and react in the way you desire.

VI.

As a footnote to these three basic rules, remember humor--even if it is a grim practical joke that only you can afford to smile at. Humor is often the test of a good psychological operation, since humor is constructed on the frailties of mankind--and skilled playing on these frailties increases the effectiveness of the psychological weapon. Those of you who knew Admiral Miles' operations in China should recall the risks his Chinese agents took to wall-paint slogans poking fun at the Japanese. In some instances, the main motivation of volunteers who risked death doing this was the appeal of playing a prank.

VII.

As a second footnote to these three basic rules, remember and honor the old adage that "actions speak louder than words". Psychological operations aren't much good if you say one thing earnestly, and then prove that you didn't really mean it by acting otherwise. There are times when troop behavior, military courtesy, true discipline, will speak far more loudly than any leaflets or broadcasts. There is no substitute for living your beliefs.

In other words, pay attention to actions. About this time a year ago, the Royal Lao Government was vying with the Communist-controlled Neo Lao Hoc Xat for the support of villagers in the muongs. Part of the government's program was to bring pure water to the villages--and to this end set about digging wells industriously. I heard of one village, not far from Vientiane, which had one of these wells dug--and had been waiting patiently for the government to install a pump. When it wasn't forthcoming, the local Neo Lao Hoc Xat started digging another well right next to this one. You can be sure that the Communists had a pump ready for this well. So, what good would government

3

peakers, leaflets, and broadcasts do in telling these villagers that the government was their friend--when the other side proved its friendship by its action?

Now, here I am, starting to illustrate already. So, it's time to give you
some case histories. These will be necessarily brief. They all concern
operations against the Communist enemy by military men of the Free World.

VIII.

The first two are dated in the Fall of 1954. The place is the Tonkin delta
in the north of Vietnam.

The Background. An armistice, known to us as the Geneva Agreement
of 1954, had ended the 8-year Franco-Vietminh war. The Agreement split
Vietnam into two countries at the 17th Parallel, the northern going to the
Communist Vietminh, the southern to the Free Vietnamese. Armed forces,
which had been in conflict throughout the country, were to be evacuated to their
respective areas according to a detailed plan, ending in 300 days, in May 1955.
In June 1956, the Vietnamese would hold a plebiscite to vote on the future of
their country.

The Problem: Reflective thought was given to what the Communists had
in mind when they dictated this armistice. One conclusion was that they expected
to win the proposed plebiscite in 1956. The 17th Parallel split Vietnam to give
the Communists the majority of the population, and Communist control methods
could assure that voting would be favorable to them. As the Free Vietnamese
said, "In June 1956, we commit suicide." Thus, it was imperative to shift
the majority vote from the Communist controls in the North to the Free South.
To do this conclusively, nearly 2-million people would have to move. The
problem was: to make people whose families had been on the same land for
generations leave it for an unknown land among strangers many hundreds of
miles to the south.

The Action: Many psychological operations were carried out, to give
these people who desired freedom, but who loved their native soil, a last push
to leave it before the Communists--whom they had cause to fear--took over.
Two examples, selected from many, will illustrate psywar techniques. The
first is a rumor campaign. The second is black, or seemingly done by the
enemy.

The Vietnamese Army G-5, or "Morale Action", had an armed propoaganda
company in the Hanoi area. They were trained in methods of spreading rumors
in markets and other public places. A story was given, broken into a series of
anecdotes which the listeners would put together for themselves and thus come
to their own conclusion. The anecdotes included hints of the presence of
Chinese soldiers in a village, the public execution of some of the men of the

4

village, hints of sexual relations imposed on the women, and finally, a Chinese unit name. The end conclusion would be that the hated Chinese, in this case the Communist Chinese, really controlled the puppet Vietminh and had already moved a ChiCom division into a village north of Hanoi, and were acting like just the brutes the people expected them to be. Memories of Chinese occupation in 1945 were fresh. The rumors took hold because they were just what the people expected. Several weeks afterwards, Hanoi, Hai Duong, and Haiphong were buzzing with reports of the presence of 3 to 5 ChiCom divisions in Vietnam. People had simply embellished the G-5 rumor operation in the re-telling.

The black operation was based upon a fake Vietminh leaflet. The leaflet was most convincing. It appeared to be from the secret Vietminh security organization in Hanoi--in language, in local printing, in local paper, in tone. It asked the local inhabitants to remain in Hanoi, reassured that there would be an orderly take-over by the Vietminh, asked residents and shopkeepers to inventory all personal belongings, told how to list these properly, including money, and then became overly reassuring that the Communists would respect these personal belongings. Of course, this reassurance sparked the recollection that the Communists sure as hell didn't respect personal property. The effectiveness of this black leaflet, and similar ones, was such that the Vietminh used radio broadcasts to denounce them as fakes. However, the leaflets were so true to style that most of the Communists inside Hanoi laughed at these broadcasts, thinking they were secret French or Vietnamese efforts to discredit the Party's work, and the leaflets remained effective for weeks.

The third example is dated in late 1954. The place is Cochin-China, hundreds of miles south of Hanoi.

The background is much the same as given in the first two examples. Only, this time, it concerns the Vietminh forces which were in the South or Free Vietnam, and who would have to be evacuated by Communist shipping to Vietminh territory north of the 17th Parallel. Polish ships were used for this, embarking the Vietminh initially at Cap St. Jacques. A look at these ships revealed that they were American Liberty ships given to the Soviets in World War II and apparently not painted since they left U.S. shipyards originally. They had a rusty, trampish look. And, at the same time, the Communists had just heard that the U.S. Navy, and other Free World Navies, were coming in to give a sea lift to refugees from the North. The initial Communist propaganda to counter this was to charge that these Naval forces were going to be used to block the Communist transports. Let me remark here that this Communist tactic was impulsive and amateurish--and just begged to be clobbered.

The problem, of course, was to cause as many of the non-Party followers of the Communist Vietminh to remain south of the 17th Parallel

5

192

in Free Vietnam, as possible. There had to be an upset of Communist calculations at Geneva on how many people they would have under their control for the planned 1956 Plebiscite.

The Action. Among a number of psychological operations taken to keep the followers pegged down in the South where they could be educated later, one was outstanding. This was a black leaflet which purported to be instructions from the Evacuation Organization of the Communist Party. It was done in authentic Communist style. Paper, printing, and language all rang true. It was distributed in all Vietminh evacuation areas in Cochin-China by G-6, the clandestine Service of the Vietnamese Army, whose agents travelled widely in enemy-held zones. It listed the personal gear that people could bring with them, urging that warm clothes be brought along, not only for the notably cold winters of Tonkin, but also warm clothes would be useful to those who naturally would volunteer to join the patriots building the railroad in China. As a foot-note at the bottom, there was an angry denial that evacuees would be unsafe on the voyage north. The Red Navy would see to that. Not only that, but all evacuees would be kept safe, well below deck, so that Imperialist fighter air-craft couldn't strafe them. This scary picture, which previous Communist propaganda had helped, really came into sharp focus when the evacuees reached Cap St. Jacques and saw the rusty, raffish transports awaiting them, and pictured themselves trapped below deck in what looked like floating coffins. Word spread quickly. There was a really significant refusal to go North, including sizeable units of Vietminh combat forces.

IX.

The fourth example is dated in late 1950. The place is in Central Luzon, in the Philippines.

The Background. The Communist Huks were reaching the climax of their savage and bloody attempt to overthrow the Philippine Government by force. Terroristic raids on towns were frightening to government officials— and rightly so, as proved by the numbers of officials pulled out of their houses at night and executed in the street by the Huks, and the wanton butchery of unarmed civilians. It was a time of frightening cruelty. The provincial governors demanded that the Philippine Army garrison all the towns in the trouble area. The governors, and the votes they represented, had a big say with the President. So, the Philippine Army was under immense political pressure to keep spread out in necessarily small garrisons all over the map. Yet, the situation demanded that the Army concentrate into striking forces that could hit the enemy in real effective strength. This meant pulling garrisons out of the towns to get the troops with which to build such forces.

The Problem. Among the many measures being taken at the time, it was decided to see if some psychological interdiction would work. The problem was:

193

to make the Huks move away from an area where they were threatening a town, and thus free the Army troops garrisoning the town to be concentrated with other troops into a Combat Team.

The Action. It was known that the Huks were coming into town secretly at night, from their hillside camp in the nearby jungle. They would visit townspeople, who had a secret Communist government--the real government to the people was this secret night one--court trials, punishments, taxes, even for marriages. Thus, it was known that the Huks and the people talked to each other.

The psychological operation was based upon these known facts, plus known Filipino superstitions. Selected Philippine Army officers and men carried out the operation.

Rumors were spread, in markets, barber-shops, and other public places--in segmented anecdotes which a listener would finally put together for himself. The stories were based upon the reputed sayings of a noted soothsayer in Ilocos Norte, an old lady who had predicted the death of President Roxas. She was now predicting that men with evil in their hearts would be the victims of the local and terrifying vampire. The Huk jungle area was named as the locale in the noted soothsayer's prediction. A man would be foolish to believe this--but then, who knows? Roxas hadn't believed her and look what happened to him.

This story was planted all one day. The first night the Army stayed put, to permit the Huks to come to town, and hear this superstitious story from the townspeople. The next night, an Army patrol was staked out on the trail to town. When the Huks came down it, cautiously, the last man was silently grabbed by the patrol. When the Huks were out of the vicinity, the captured Huk was held down, two holes punched in his throat, held up by the heels, and drained of blood. The body was carefully placed back on the trail. The returning Huks found the body. The vampire evidence was compelling. The Huks deserted their strongly held jungle area before dawn.

With the departure of this Huk threat, the troops could leave town-- without political repercussions.

X.

The last example is in mid-1951. Again, the place is Luzon, the Philippines.

The Background. By mid-1951, the Philippine Army under the personal, direct, and dynamic leadership of the Secretary of National Defense, Ramon Magsaysay, had wrested the military initiative from the Huks. Until then, it had all been a crash emergency, with time for little more than patchwork measures on constructing the political base required for victory over the Communists. It's not enough to be against Communism; you have to be for something.

The Huks had recruited much of their strength and their huge, sympathetic following by exploiting the 1949 Presidential Election in the Philippines. The overwhelming majority of Filipinos, fanned by Communist propaganda, believed that it had been a crooked election, that the elected Administration had come to power through cheating at the ballot box. In effect, this made a fine Constitution and an enlightened Electoral Code just scraps of paper instead of the firm political tenets in which a man could believe. The Huk said: your ballot isn't counted; join us and use a gun to get a new government; it's the only way.

Magsaysay saw the situation clearly as one in which the military could make no further gains, would simply be forced to continue the killing of its brother Filipinos, unless the Philippines Constitution and the Electoral Code were brought back to life for all Filipinos. The General Staff and the Commission on Elections agreed with him. A number of the key members of the Administration, including the President, were out of the country. The Electoral Commissioners, quietly but legally, asked the Armed Forces for help in making the November 1951 election a clean one. This was a by-election, for a third of the Senators and for local officials. Plans were made to use troops, reinforced by ROTC students, to insure protection of candidates and electorate, truly secret balloting, and an honest count.

The Problem. In this atmosphere of a pending proof of which is the better way to change a government--with the bullet or with the ballot--there was the opportunity to strongly discredit the Communist leaders who advocated armed rebellion as the only way. The problem, then, was to discredit them effectively among their large following.

The Action. A number of actions were carried out successfully during the 1951 Election period. Perhaps the key one, however, was a black psychological operation which was closely keyed to the plans of the Commission on Elections and the Armed Forces. Incidentally, this psychological operation was done so skillfully that it took the Politburo a year and a half of careful, dogmatic analysis to figure out what had happened in this particular attack on it.

A small Communist propaganda cell, on the northern outskirts of Manila, had been penetrated by a special intelligence unit. A leaflet was carefully prepared, using Communist typewriter, mimeograph and paper. It was so introduced that the cell believed it was its own. The leaflet called for a boycott of the election, pointing out in strong terms the cheating in the 1949

8

lection, and predicting that a disgusted electorate would join the Huks' "armed struggle" after the election and that the best way to ensure this was to maintain aloofness from the corrupt election practices of the capitalists. The leaflet reached the Politburo in the hills, who rebuked the Agitprop cell for independent action in propaganda, but then adopted the line itself. Communist leaders, including Huk regional and squadron commanders, pushed this line hard throughout the provinces and became closely identified with it. It looked like a golden opportunity to them in the bleak days of the turn of military fortune.

Then came Election Day. The 1951 election was remarkably honest—the plan of the Armed Forces and the Commission on Elections had worked. In fact, the opposition candidates won overwhelmingly against Administration candidates—a fact which the electorate took as open proof of a clean election. While the Philippines electorate was awakening to the fact that its Constitution and its Electoral Code were live, working documents for patriots to live by, the rank and file of the Communist Huk movement were awakening to the fact that their leaders had been dead wrong about a political fact. It was entirely possible, as the Army was pointing out in its intensive psychological campaign, that the Communist leaders were wrong in all their political thinking. Thousands of Huk military and civilian supporters left the Huk Movement. This major defeat marked the beginning of the end for the Huks.

XI.

Now, to sum up.

Note that the case histories given you were thumb-nail sketches of psychological operations conducted by national armed forces against an armed enemy. They were selected to give you a taste of the variety of actions which can be taken against the Communist enemy, who not only fights "with no holds barred", but who makes coordinated use of political, economic, and military weapons when he fights us.

Note that each action was a necessary one—that it fitted in solidly with what had to be done at that historic moment. This seeing of the important necessities of the moment, recognizing them, understanding them—and not frittering away energy and resources on side issues which look so attractive to the many who only see the surface—this is a fundamental "must" for success.

Secondly, note that in each of these examples, it was first determined exactly what each operation should cause people to do. The desired end result was clearly thought out first.

And thirdly, note that each operation fitted into local acceptance--in tone, in its message, and in the medium used.

One final point should be made. The Asian men who carried out these operations were dedicated patriots. They had to be, because in these and similar operations, they pledged their lives towards the success of what they did--without expectation of reward other than having a country in which their children could grow up as free men. This, too, is our bond of brotherhood with them. It prompts me to conclude this talk with a personal observation: the best American psychological operators I have known have had a deep spiritual kinship with our unpaid Continental troops at Valley Forge, with the men on both sides in the Sunday morning woods at Shiloh, and, yes, with the "Thomasites" of this century, the teachers sent by the War Department to start free public schools throughout the Philippines, often at risk of life. This kinship carries them past the pitfalls of a pragmatism which is merely shallow selfishness--and keeps them atune to the far deeper, moving, true objectives of the American people. These are the objectives which warmly bond together the freedom loving people throughout the world and are the great strength which gives meaning to all of our actions bringing the eventual defeat of the Communists.

10